Tight Lines
Nigel Williams
2005

JUST WILLIAMS

by Nige Williams

First Published 2005

Published by Lucebaits Publishing
The Tackle Shop, Bridge Road,
Gainsborough, Lincolnshire.
DN21 1JS

ISBN 0-9543526-1-0

Acknowledgements

My obsession with fishing began at a very early age when Granddad Herbert Clarke first introduced me to this wonderful sport and I began reading Mr Crabtree books by Bernard Venables. There has never been a lull in my enthusiasm since but I would like to acknowledge in this book those who have inspired me in my pike fishing career. In the early days John Watson and Eddie Turner (ET) were my heroes. I am known as a travelling angler and Des Taylor must take sole credit for this as he encouraged me to explore the UK's pike potential and not just sit in my own back yard. Neville Fickling for all the knowledge I've gained over the years through his articles, the endless fishing trips (especially Ladybower) and of course without him there would be no 'Just Williams'. Fishing is also about having a good time with your mates and therefore Gary Banks deserves a medal for putting up with me!! Lastly, behind this pike angler is a family that supports me every step of the way so all my love and thanks must go to Dianne, Jennie and Ross.

Contents

Not every weekend could be spent in Wales so he would travel to Bridgenorth on the Severn with his best mate David Kay. There they would fish for barbel and chub. Readers should note that the Severn was a different river in those days. The barbel were still establishing themselves and it was a case of quantity rather than quality. The Severn then was a noted match fishing venue.

Nige wasn't destined to pursue an academic career, leaving school at the age of 16 with 5 GCEs. His initial plan was to be a bricklayer, but he spotted an advert in a shop window. He went to work for Fenwicks of Wolverhampton a fishing tackle and gun shop. He worked there for 7 years as a shop assistant. Then he left there and went to work for Ron Baker, a match angler who at the time held the 3 hour match record on the Severn with something like 78lb of chub. Sadly Ron died leaving Nige to run the business as manager for the last year... Then he bought the business still at 67 Lowe Street, Whitmore Reans for £9000 and took on the lease. At the time they used to sell 600 pints of casters a week! He was the first person to sell dry casters (still alive) and anglers travelled from far and wide to buy them. He then moved to 210 Newhampton Road West. There he remained from 1983 to 2003 when he sold the business and the property. The thing that clinched the decision to sell was being unable to find the staff to run the business so Nige could go fishing two days a week. He now works as a Consultant for Masterline, is a columnist for Anglers Mail and does some TV work with Sky Television. He also does a limited amount of guiding on the River Severn and Lake Windermere.

He has a number of strong views about angling at the moment. In the 2002/2003 season he won the Fox Cup in a competition run by Anglers Mail. In addition to the cup he also walked away with a cheque for a cool £3000. He won this for six thirty pound plus pike in a calendar year. He was however unable to make any impact on the Angling Times specimen fish competition the Drennan Cup. Nige believes that no pike angler is ever going to be able to win the Drennan cup simply because it is strongly biased towards barbel, chub and carp. While he has considerable respect for some of the well known anglers who do consistently well with these species, Nige would argue that because these species are long lived compared to pike and they are recaught many times each season, it is always easier for the barbel, carp or chub angler to put in a good performance over the season. The pike angler also has less time to make his mark in a season. Very few really big pike come out during the period March to October, while barbel, chub and carp can turn up at any time. (Except of course the close season on rivers). His own personal best performance in the Drennan Cup was a third place and that was with a 40-12, a 30 pounder and a 6-1 eel. He would have thought that a 40lb pike alone would have been enough to come third and another thirty might clinch it. Interestingly when Neville Fickling caught his 41-06 pike, he had a 32-06 the next day. He came second in the Drennan Cup to Greg Buxton's 14lb barbel. So perhaps the Drennan Cup has always been biased towards fish without teeth.

It may be being unkind to the people at Drennan, but Nige certainly feels that two or three years ago this bias became even worse. He is also convinced that a lot of the chub,

The Fox Cup

barbel and carp anglers voted for each other. The Drennan cup is voted for by people who have previously won a Drennan award and of course it is likely that more of them are carp, chub and barbel anglers! A thirty pound plus pike is a more worthy fish than a 15lb barbel or a 6lb chub and it galls Nige that so few anglers won a Drennan award with a 35lb plus pike from Blithfield. Someone at AT must have decided that 35 pounders on lures were as common as muck. This is clearly not the case; you only have to look at the situation in 2003/4.

On another subject he regrets the passing of the old close season, but is now baffled as to why it has been retained on rivers. It really should be abolished completely. When asked if this might impact on pike stocks he feels that most pike anglers would not go until October and then pack up in March. If the pressure on pike did increase it would be easy enough for fishery managers and angling clubs to impose their own close season.

Outside of fishing he has little time for other activities but he has been a keen participant in sub aqua and also enjoys off road motorcycling with his son Ross and making lots of noise!

There's a dream that lifts
me from my bed,
Takes me to the waters edge.
For a boy doesn't decide to fish,
He sees the water and is drawn to it.
Every angler knows of a place;
The walk to which sets the pulse to race
The sound, the flow, the still, the depth;
The sight of which can take your breath
Where imagination and reality meet.
Hallowed ground beneath your feet.

How quiet but full of life
this world can be,
How much this worlds a part of me.
And when you finally cast an eye,
Make believe where the fish do lie;
Somewhere on it's watery bed
A giant of giants is raising it's head.
It's a fire that burns down deep inside
Keeps me warm under wintry skies.
That fire is stoked and at it's best
When the fish of my dreams is in the net.

T. C. BROWN
2005

THE BASICS

Probably the countries top match angler Bob Nudd is know for the meticulous way he prepares his fishing tackle. While I neither need nor wish to be Bob Nudd, I have my own degree of organisation that demands a degree of perfection. What I have to contend with is not the fine details of a delicate rig, but a much more widespread range of tackle. This can range from a trace and hooks to a bait boat. Everything has to work to as near maximum efficiency as I can manage. There is little point turning up on a water and finding out that I cannot put my baits where I want them. Losing a fish because of some defect has to be avoided at all costs, because with my track record of having the biggest fish on a first visit a duff trace could be a disaster. The same applies to bait, I need to source the best and present it in a manner which will not deter the fish I am after. I am going to look here in detail at everything I use to catch pike.

TACKLE

RODS

My first pike rod was acquired for me by my parents using their Green Shield stamps. (Remember them!) It was a horrible bamboo thing with pink Syntox rings. Luckily things have improved since then.

Like most pike anglers I have been through a lot of different rods over the years. I would hope by now that I have a pretty good idea of what constitutes the ideal pike rod. For bait fishing it has to be able to do two things. One it has to cast the bait out. Secondly it has to have sufficient backbone so that when you wind down and pull into a fish the hooks have the maximum pressure applied to them when the fish tries to eject the bait. At that point the hooks go home. It amazes me how much nonsense is written about hooking pike. We have had some pundits claiming that you have to give two or three sharp strikes. Then there was the traditional side ways strike as advocated by Mr. Crabtree. This tactic was still being advocated in the sixties and seventies. No-one seemed to realise that no matter how you attempted to hook a pike, the line of pressure was going to be the same regardless of any angles you could conjure up. You can simulate the whole process when standing on the bank and getting a mate to hold a bait (without hooks!) while you do a variety of “strikes”. The different rods I have gone through were a fraction of what was available at the time. It seemed impossible to arrive at the ideal rod quickly. The way pike angler’s fish and the size of baits may also have varied over the years and this will have a bearing on the rods for the job.

My first rods were Northwestern SS5s and SS4s. These were built from blanks, something most pike anglers did in those days. Both were glass fibre rods with hard chrome rings and a 2lb test curve. The SS5 was through action, rather heavy and 11ft long. I used that for my bank fishing. The SS4 was 10ft long and similar in all other respects to the SS4. It is funny to think that in those days we thought these rods were really nice to fish with. We caught lots of pike and it felt good having them bend right down to the butt. However in those early days baits were relatively small, long casting was not required and the pike rarely reached double figures.

Then in the late seventies Northwestern launched the PK2 and the PK3 which were 23/4lb test of 10ft and 11ft respectively. These were much more powerful rods. Because I was in the trade I was in a good position to get these rods quite cheaply and of course I again made them up myself. The advent of these rods saw me catching a few better fish to 18lb and now my bait choice was wider and my casting distance had improved. These rods were poker like and I had many happy days trying to cast my baits off. However if you wanted to fish half mackerel baits at any range you certainly wouldn't be able to do it with an SS5.

Then the first carbon fibre blanks appeared in the early eighties. Now we had rods which would do the job, but also felt quite good to use. You only have to pick up an old glass rod to wonder how we put up with them. Yet in the end a bean pole will catch a fish, however the entertainment value of such a rod is nil. You only have to look at the split cane rods which existed in the sixties to see how bad things could be. These new carbon rods were 12ft 3lb test and instead of dreaming of casting 70 yards with a half mackerel we could now do it. Being in the tackle trade I saw a lot of new products and if I liked them I sometimes gave them a try. Selling my old rods in the shop I ended up using the original 12ft Daiwa Whisker Kevlar rods. These were slimmer than anything that had gone before and probably a little overrated in their test curve their only problem was that the gold coloured rings only lasted six months, but luckily because I kept changing rods I never found this out. Then I tried the 13ft Whiskers which were a more powerful rod and realised like many other people that 13ft rods were a pain in the neck because they wouldn't fit into a lot of cars. Luckily the rings had improved by this stage. Because I did not like Duplon I changed all the handles to cork. When I think about it I spent an awful amount of time fiddling about with my rods! This was mainly to fill the empty days in a fishing tackle shop that was very quiet in winter.

Next I went what many would consider to be completely barmy I went telescopic mad. DAM had brought out a 12ft 3lb telescopic rod which on inspection seemed to be perfectly up to the job especially as now I was using a radio controlled boat for all my long distance work. The advantage of a telescopic rod is that it takes up little space and you can set up and pack up very quickly. They were also brilliant for poaching. I used to stick a piece of foam in the tip ring and when I had a run it pulled the top sections of the rod out. In those days it was two rods only so I could keep the extra rod under my chair. The only snag with these rods was that I used to break half a dozen a year. Luckily replacing sections was a straight forward process though whether this was a good advert for telescopic rods I'm not sure.

Next came Normark 12ft Titans, all 3lb test. These were a powerful through action rod. They were rung up for carp fishing so the first job was to re ring them. They only had 5 single leg rings so I replaced these with 9 Fuji rings. I extended the butt by 4 inches because the reel seat was too low on the blank. Amazingly I've used them for four years and not broken one. A tribute to a blank if there ever was one!

For boat fishing which does not require long casting there was nothing suitable available. My initial efforts involved 11ft $2\frac{3}{4}$ Northwestern carbons cut down to 10 foot 6ins, 4 inches off the tip and 2 inches off the butt. This gave a through action, but powerful rod. In the early 90s I had some Centuary Composite blanks which again I cut down from 11ft to 10ft 6ins again with cork handles because they held better in boat rod

Ross with a 25-04 from Chew.

rests. These were then sold and Masterline who I now work for supplied me with some Voodoo 12ft 2 $\frac{3}{4}$lb test rods which I again stripped down, took 6 inches off the tip and 9 inches off the top of the butt section and used this off cut to produce a spigot rather than leave as an over slide join. The result is a very powerful rod about $3\frac{3}{4}$lb test. The advantage of this type of rod is that you can stop a big fish going under the boat and coming into contact with the anchor ropes. Using short powerful rods is a lot easier to net fish on your own. Last but not least when I'm in my own boat these rods fold up nicely to fit in my own cuddy which is only a quarter size. As I write I have designed a series of rods for Masterline which I hope will define pike fishing rods for the immediate future. There will be a 10ft lure rod for fixed spool use, casting up to 3oz using 50lb braid. This is for those who do not wish to use short rods and multipliers. Then there is the 10ft 6ins boat rod built around the design I have already mentioned, but not quite as powerful with a nice through action. For Fenland type fishing an 11ft 2 $\frac{1}{4}$lb test rod for situations where distance and big baits are not required. There will be a 12ft 3lb test livebait/deadbait rod and a 12ft 3¼lb drifter and long range rod. All the rods fold ring to ring exactly in half for easy carriage.

In my garage I keep up to 14 sets of rods and reels ready made so that I can be ready to go at the drop of a hat. Currently my rod armoury comprises two lure rods, four dead-baiting set ups, four boat rods and four river/ fen set ups. This may seem excessive, but it saves having to constantly retackle rods. When you have to make snap decisions as to where you are going at 4 in the morning the last thing you need is having to get up half an hour earlier to retackle. The price of fishing tackle has gone down in recent years so having a large collection of rods is something most keen pike anglers can afford.

I am a great believer in using the right tools for the job when pike fishing. Some fellow anglers look at my rods and think they are over powerful. However if you are using baits of 12oz to a 1lb you are not going to hook anything unless you wind down fast and bend hard into the pike. It is rather like lure fishing with big lures and big hooks. You will hook pike better with a stiff powerful rod rather than with a rubber rod!

REELS

Reels for pike fishing have to endure everything we throw at them. We sometimes cast weights that would be more suited to beach casting tackle. The size of fish we catch is greater than most coarse anglers expect to catch. While a carp angler's tackle spends much of it's time doing nothing, pike fishing is more active and therefore places greater strain on a reel. Reeling in deadbaits and heavy leads from long range imposes great strain on the spool and shaft of the reel. So all we demand from a pike reel is that it puts up with everything we throw at it, requires minimum maintenance and works in an idiot proof matter so when we anglers make a mistake that mistake does not end up being terminal.

Like most young anglers from the seventies I started off using Intrepid reels. I remember mine being a Black Prince while my mate David Kay who had more money than me could afford a Super Twin! The first fixed spool reels I ever used for my serious pike fishing were Mitchell 300s and one 306. The 300s were the best reels available in the 70s and early 80s. They had gearing which was smooth, but also resistant to the reel over running if left without the anti reverse off. The 306 was simply a larger reel, designed for light saltwater fishing. Just like the glass rods that we thought were pretty good, when the first modern fixed spool reels appeared we realised that the Mitchell 300 was not quite as good as we thought. The 300 had a number of faults; worst of all was the habit of the line getting behind the spool. Also the bale arm was strictly automatic so you couldn't close it by hand. Bale arm springs expired with boring regularity and the shallow plastic spools if loaded too tightly with line tended to explode. The Mitchell 300 was probably responsible for more people learning to backwind than anything else. The front clutch was not very good, but luckily when you let the reel handle go when surprised by a fast moving fish, the inbuilt inertia of the gearing system prevented an over run.

It was not long before ABU brought in their series of stern drag reels, first the 444A and then the much better Cardinal Series such as the 55 and the 57. These had skirted spools a stern drag and top quality gearing. Unfortunately they too suffered bale arm spring problems despite having two of them. Some 57s bale arms snapped over on the cast and the line lay on the narrow spool was worse than on the 300 which up until then was still better than any other reel. Nearly all pike anglers of this period went through the same progression with reels.

Because I was doing a lot of boat fishing then, I moved on to multipliers. There were only the ABU Ambassador 6000 series worth considering in those days. They were well machined, had a level wind and they had a clicker you could use when they were in free spool mood. This meant that when boat fishing you could hear the line being pulled off of the reel. You could also fish thicker line with them more easily than you could with a fixed spool. It should be remembered that 18lb Sylcast was like rope in those days. Greasing a line using ET grease was also easier with a multiplier. The clutch was perfect; unfortunately the line retrieve was so slow you struggled to keep in touch with a fast moving fish. We also had to contend with the fact that all these reels were right hand wind. Despite this I used these reels for a number of years, always being extra careful when trying to cast light baits into the wind. Generally not advisable!

Then out of the blue came the revolution of the Shimano Baitrunners. Here were reels with skirted spool, a good front drag, a bale arm that didn't go wrong and most important of all a free spool mechanism which allowed the angler to fish with a closed bale arm while line could still be taken. It seems funny today when there are dozens of different Baitrunner type reels how we ever managed to do without them. The first Shimanos were the chunky 3500 and 4500 Seaspins and as soon as I saw them I had to have. I never managed to break one and they served me well for 4 years. Their only slight defect was once again a poor line lay. Then as luck would have it I obtained some sponsorship from ABU and I was re-equipped with 656BWs. These were a copy of the Shimano, but unfortunately an inferior product. I managed to break the bale arms, shatter the gearing and broke the side casing of one. Such destructive abilities have never again been seen in angling! Then Browning supplied me with four reels which were again bait runner types and they lasted one season. Enough said about those. It soon became clear to me that we had entered the era of the disposable reel!

ABU then came up with some better free spool reels which I kept for a couple of years. Then I went back to the Shimanos with the Seaspins and also the new 10000GTs. These new Shimanos have so far survived my attentions. The Seaspins have remained more or less the same ever since and it is generally agreed amongst many anglers that they are one of the best reels ever produced. Recent updates have improved the main axle which is stronger, the line lay is slightly better and the clutch is much improved. On the 10000s the line lay is the best I have ever seen. On the multiplier front I still have the 6500s, but for lure fishing I have left hand wind reels. Masterline Toothy Critter reels have served me well for the past year. There is enough spool capacity to get plenty of heavy braid on for casting or trolling.

LINE

There is one thing you can be sure of in pike fishing and that is that a line of inadequate strength or of poor quality it is going to cost you fish. Not only is it bad news for the angler, but in some cases it can lead to the death of the fish you are after. When I first started pike fishing the choices of line was fairly limited. I used 11lb Sylcast which in those days was probably underated and broke at above 11lb. It was horribly thick though and springy. For all that it was reliable and many specialist anglers caught a lot of big fish of many species using it. Interestingly the brand has totally dissappeared now. We also tried to be able to afford Platil Extra Strong which was one of the early extra thin monos. We used it in 12lb, but generally had to settle for the ordinary Platil.

The advent of braid was to relegate monofilament lines to secondary uses. My first braid was ABU Excellent in 30lb breaking strain. This had the diameter of 8lb mono. The difference in casting was amazing. There was also the non stretch property which made hooking pike easier and of course it floated eliminating the chore of having to grease a mono line when drifting. It was bright blue in colour which helped in finding where your line was. This saved a lot of tangles. An early lesson most of had to learn the hard way was not to overfill the spool. To do so led to a wonderful cast one time and a horrible birds nest the next. The golden rule then and now with braid is to slightly under fill a fixed spool reel. There were also some interesting fun and games for the unwary who attempted to tie braid directly to the reel spool only to find that the entire spool full of braid rotates on its own. A short length of mono loaded on the spool first or a dab of superglue prevented this problem.
Playing a big fish on braid was a totally new experience. I have always preferred to use the clutch with braid though it is quite possible to backwind if that is your preferred method of playing fish. There are a lot different braids about at the moment, but my requirements are fulfilled by the following. For bank fishing with fixed spool reels I currently use Cortland Spectrum in 35lb breaking strain and I can get 300m on my reels which should be enough for anyone and I do not have to resort to big pit type reels. For boat fishing I have to step up to 50lb breaking strain simply because a lot more can go wrong when afloat. Again I'm using Cortland. For my fixed spool lure fishing it is 35lb Cortland again. This gives me enhanced casting which when the fish are well out and helps also when in competition with anglers using multipliers and heavier braid it enabling me to cover more water.

On the multiplier setup so much of my fishing uses quite big lures some of which are expensive, costing as much as £13 to £17 a go. With the number of snags in some waters and the tendency for some pike to live near the bottom, lure fishing would become too expensive unless heavy braid was used to enable lures to be recovered. My choice at the moment is again Cortland this time in 80lb breaking strain. Different braids have different diameters for the same breaking strain. Where abrasion is not a problem it is sensible to go for as fine a line as possible. It just makes casting a lot easier. A finer braid also allows a lure to work deeper than a thick braid when trolling. Knots need to be different for braid and I have always used the double Grinner knot with the braid twice through the eye of the swivel.

Braids tend to last longer than monos. Usually the first ten yards will need to be cut off from time to time. You can generally tell when this needs to be done. The line starts to look a bit hairy. It will still be strong enough to land a horse, but as a precaution should be disposed of thoughtfully.

TRACE WIRE

Just as important as line is your trace wire. Not using some form of pike proof leader for pike fishing is plain irresponsible. When I started my choice of wire was very limited. It was either Alasticum wire or PDQ by Pegley Davies. Both were multistrand, fairly thick wires which could be stretched to take out the kinks, though it was inadvisable to do this too often. These wires were around 20 or 30lb breaking strain. They served us well then, but a lot better wires have emerged since.

Next came Drennan 7 strand in 28lb breaking strain for livebaiting which I still use today. For deadbaiting I use 30lb 49 strand VMC or the same product under another company's label. I twist my seven strand traces finishing them off neatly with a crimp. I always thread the wire through the eye of the swivel twice and the second treble is always fixed on the trace by winding around the shank of the hook. For the 49 strand I put the wire through the eye of the swivel and the treble twice and then crimp leaving the loose end of the wire just visible inside the crimp. Fox crimping pliers obtain the bests results for me.
Up traces are made of 49 strand in 50lb which is somewhat stiffer and because the pike never encounters it does not give rise to any problems in bait presentation. Because of the extra stiffness it helps to stop tangles with active livebaits.

Lure traces are made up using 50 or 100lb in 49 strand. There are some good solid traces available these days. Fox do some good traces, but care should be taken because there are also some rubbish ones about. The clips are sometimes so weak that a pike's jaws can easily open them.

HOOKS

Just like everything else hook design and quality has changed over the years. For many years I used the Partridge Outpoint, debarbing two points with forceps or long nosed pliers. Since then I've swapped and changed using all sorts. At the moment I'm on VMC Perfections. These are gun smoke in colour with a medium shank, small eye, round bend and semi barbless. They are made of carbon steel which makes them very strong and sharp. They tend to keep their point well. Sizes vary depending on bait size. For small baits I use size 4s (6s for zander). As the baits get bigger into the 1lb range we move up to size 1/0s. I never use more than two hooks on the size of baits I use. Though the way I fish is unlikely to see pike lost due to breakages, it is unwise to use more than a couple of treble hooks on a bait. To lose a bait festooned with treble hooks is almost certainly a death sentence for a pike.

For static fishing in rivers I use a special sunken float. It is hard to describe the shape of the float (it was roughly pear shaped) but the line is attached by the sharp end and from the out of the bottom. This I use for a free running paternoster rig. Andy Barker originally made them for anchored crust fishing. The diagram and photograph should explain all. The pointed end points back up towards the rod. As the river flows over the float it makes it waggle and dart about in the flow thus making your livebait work harder.

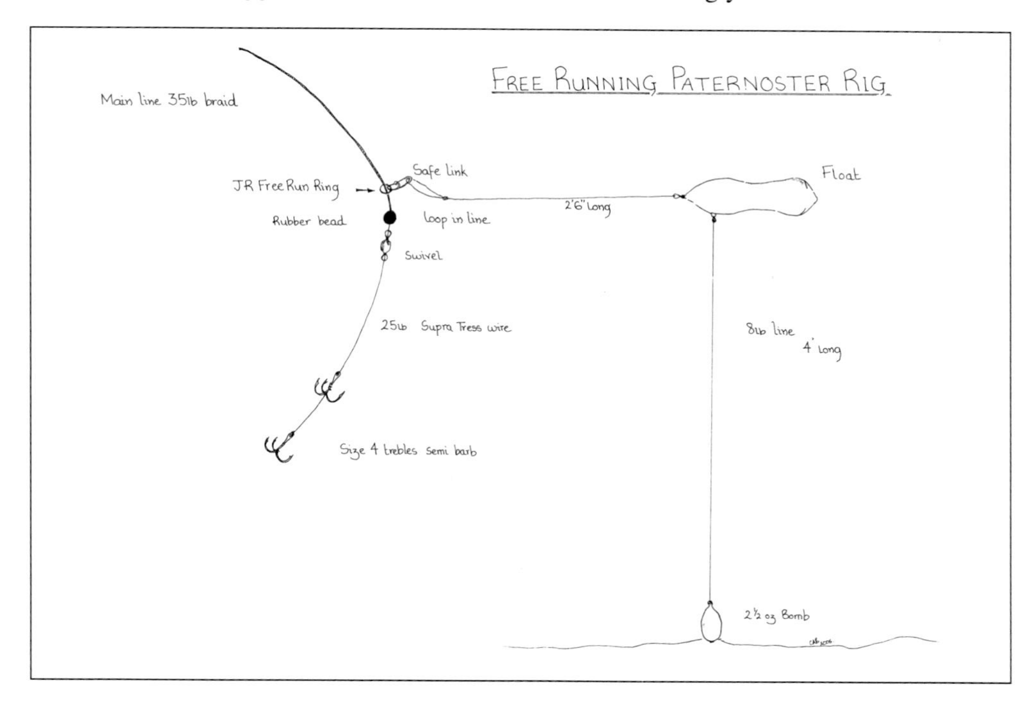

DROP OFFS.

I am a great believer in audible bite indication. Though there have been a number of drop offs on the market over the years none has been quite right. Of course when I started pike fishing it was a case of make do or mend. Before Optonics came out we used the old Heron bite alarm on its side using a drop off bobbin attached to the antennae. When the bobbin dropped off it pulled the antennae down thus setting off the alarm. The drops had to be built by myself and consisted of a knitting needle pushed through a ping pong ball. The end of the knitting needle was then sawn so as to produce a cleft into which the line could be clipped. An elastic band over this enabled me to alter the tension. The whole thing was completed with a crocodile clip attached to a piece of cord in turn attached to the end of the needle.

Regarding modern gear the Fox Micron P is nearly what I require, but to get it right I have had to doctor mine. Firstly I've changed the Terry clips on the back so it will attach to the main part of a bank stick. Then the wire to the head was not long enough, but I

Modified Fox PS alarm

Fox LXR remote heads. By the time this book is published there will also be remote PS alarms

With the remote LXR box in your pocket you will not miss even the first few bleeps from a pike

couldn't easily extend the wire so I extended the drop off bobbin itself. This I did with a short piece (4 inch) of scrap carbon blank painted fluorescent orange. This trebles the visibility of the bobbin, without increasing the weight. The clip has been replaced by a swivel and a Solar stainless steel clip which is much better at allowing drop backs with braid. As I write we still do not have a remote control drop off though one is due from Fox. If I need to have bite indication that only I can hear then I turn the P off and use the Fox DXR head with the volume down. The advantage of the remote control head is that you can bivvy up or sleep in the car, and still know if you have a run even if it's blowing a gale or raining.

DEADBAIT BOX

Mine is a standard Coleman 8 quart box with the lid filled with expanded foam. This makes the lid tight and helps to keep the baits frozen longer. For going away on long trips I have a large heavy duty polystyrene box. These can range from 10 to 25kg sizes and a week's supply of bait is easily carried in the larger box. You can get one of these for nothing when you order mail order deadbaits. You have to be sensible about how many baits you take for a session. With ten to fifteen baits in a Coleman box it would be a lucky pike angler who managed to run out of bait. If you take a bigger box and you never use all those baits you are starting to reduce your mobility.

Coleman Cool Box - big enough for a days deadbaiting, but small enough to fit in a rucksack.

LIVEBAIT CAGE AND BUCKET

To keep my livebaits I have a transporting bucket in the back of the car and a Power Bubbles which plugs into the car electrics. Another bucket into which a bait cage fits is used for carrying down the bank. A Rapala air pump is used for these short journeys. The bait cage is at the moment difficult to obtain. They were made by ET and later Gardner. They are a plastic coated mesh cage which keeps hardy baits such as trout in good condition. I bought one of the last ones available, hopefully by the time mine has expired (the last one lasted 20 years) we will be able to get them again.

The old Gardner Bait Cage which unfortunately you cannot buy at the moment

An eight foot piece of cord secures the cage to the bank using a screw in bivvy peg and a home made bungee cord keeps the lid shut. If you cannot get a livebait cage the Tackle Shop at Gainsborough sells some continental style bait buckets with a plastic cage inside. They are just big enough to be useful and keep baits better than a bait tube. Bait tubes have their uses particularly if you need to retain a large supply of bait for several days.

The choice of livebaits is these days a complex issue. The rules on moving fish have always existed, but these days it is generally frowned upon. Like many pike anglers I try to operate within the rules, but sometimes it is very difficult. Where fisheries sell baits life is so much easier. Generally baits supplied by a fishery will be trout, but sometimes coarse fish such as perch will be available. Trout are not the best baits, but they are incredibly tolerant of abrasion. This means they will keep well in a livebait cage. The only problem with trout is transporting them. They need a lot of aeration and the limit for a Power Bubbles is probably around 50 fish. The warmer the water the less oxygen can dissolve in it and the harder it is to keep trout alive. In addition at higher water temperatures, trout will be more active and will in turn need more oxygen.

In an ideal world I would have a supply of good sized carp backed up by 6 to 8oz roach. There are waters that I fish regularly where the management are quite happy to allow me to use my own carp and roach baits. Elsewhere life is not so easy. The big advantage of carp is that they are very tolerant of low oxygen levels and you can keep more of them in the same sized tank than you can trout. They are also much more tolerant of being bumped around than roach. An 8oz carp is a pretty selective bait and unless the pike are starving, you generally do not have problems with small pike.

Power Bubbles aerator with gel battery for portable use. Otherwise I either plug mine into a cigar lighter or a leisure battery

BITS AND PIECES

FORCEPS PLIERS AND CUTTER.

The nicest set of forceps I have ever come across belong to Neville Fickling, but despite my best efforts which include "I've dropped them over the side" I've not been able to pinch them from him. Luckily my Rapala forceps have proved to be quite capable of unhooking the pike that I catch. Fox pliers are useful for removing the big hooks on lures from pike. When hooks are difficult to remove Fox side cutters are useful for cutting hooks. The same applies with conventional traces and hooks when they get caught in the net.

STOPKNOTS - I always use fly line backing which is Dacron braid. To make a stop knot I use a grinner knot which is similar to the Billy Lane Knot. The advantage of the Dacron is that it never burns the line when you move it. A lot of people use a lot of power gum to achieve an inferior result. My advice on power gum is use it for something else.

WEIGHTS - For paternostering I use the cheapest 2½oz carp bomb I can find and then hammer it to death. When flattened the lead is less inclined to roll. For free roving and float trolled baits I have a number of 1½ oz leads made from cut down carp bombs which are drilled through and a piece of plastic tube inserted. A piece of silicon tube

My tackle box with all the bits and pieces I need

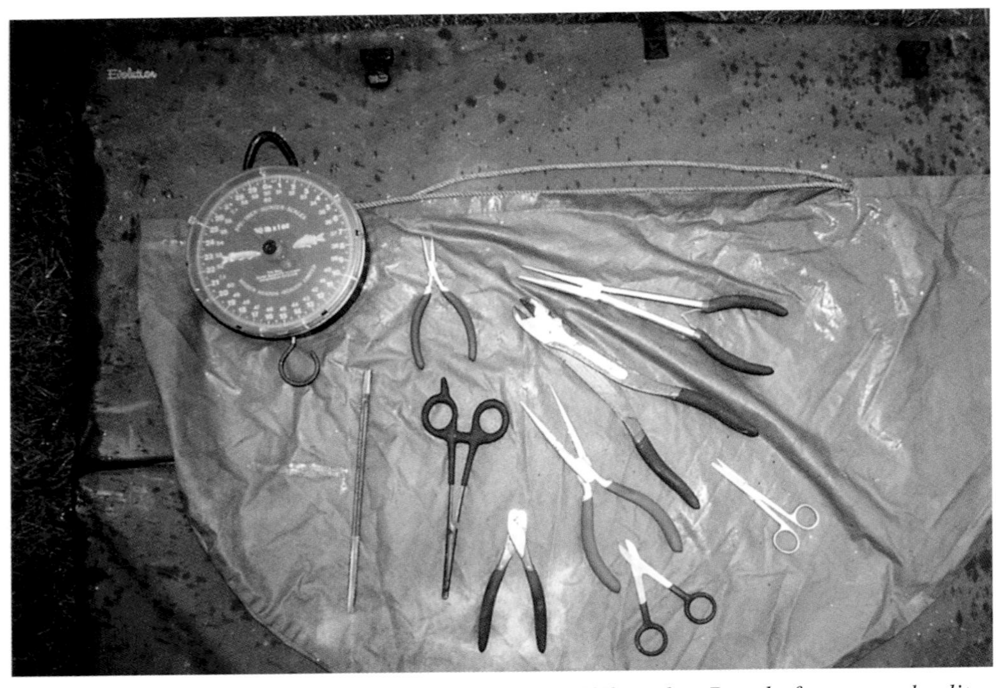

Essential kit - ET weighing sling, Reuben Heaton 60lb scales, Rapala forceps and split ring pliers, also bolt croppers, trace blades, long nose pliers and crimping pliers

Bolt croppers make short work of an awkward hook hold

Stopknot made from braid using the Billy Lane knot

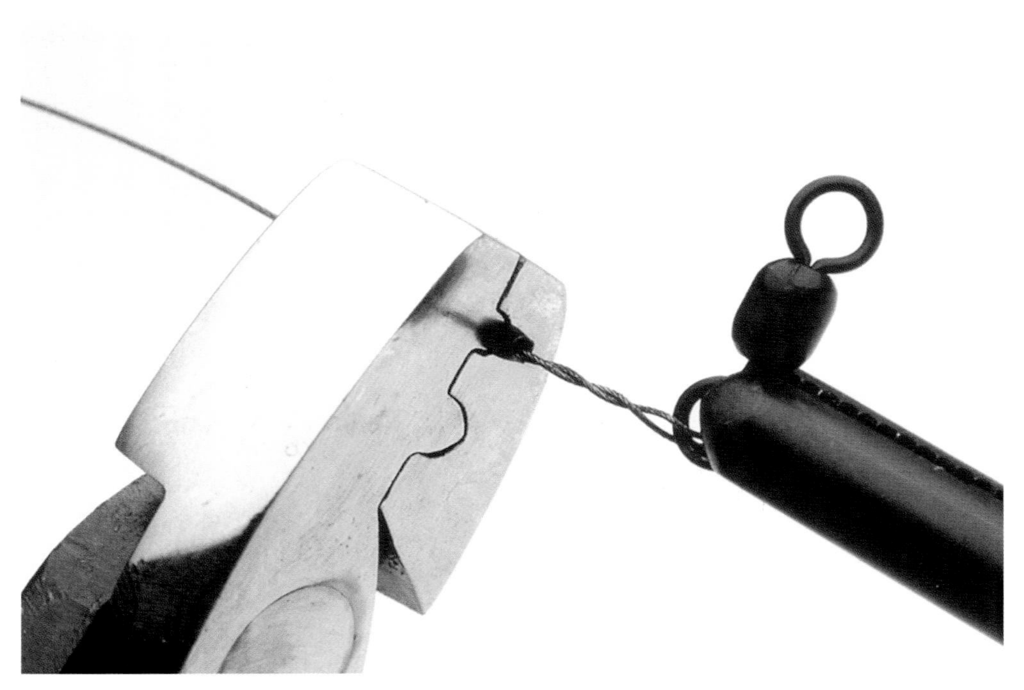

Crimping using the correct tools is fine if you are not into twisting

A selection of leads all flattened to grip better for each given weight.

over the plastic tube then allows it to be attached to the trace swivel. In this way the lead keeps the bait down where I want it.

JOHN ROBERTS PATERNOSTER BOOMS

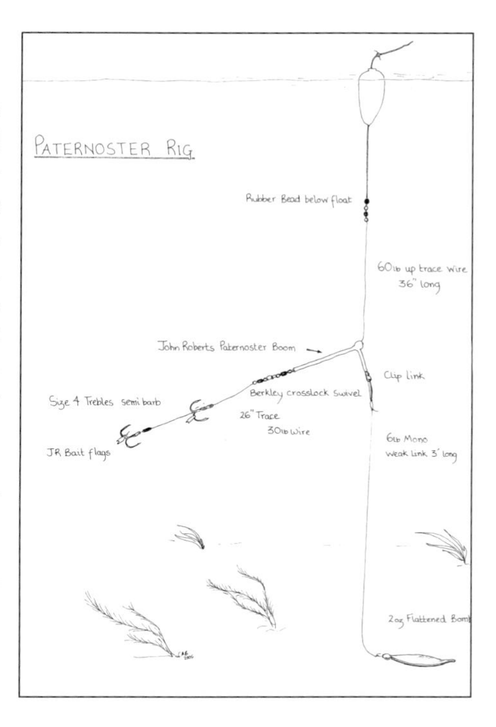

For years in my early days I only used free roving livebaits. When I discovered paternosters the rigs we used were pretty crude using a three way swivel with the trace coming off of the central swivel and the paternoster attached to the bottom swivel. A wine cork was used as a float. We used size 10 trebles because we were not confident at unhooking pike. These paternosters were fished sunken and the line was tucked under an elastic band on the rod butt. While this was good enough for runs which pulled line out of the clip it was not a lot of good for those that run towards you. I solved that problem by making my own bobbins. They were simply pilot floats with a piece of copper wire which allowed the float to be hung on the line. For fishing on the Severn I made them heavier.

Since those days the John Roberts Paternoster Boom has become an essential part of both my float paternoster rigs and also when I'm float legering. Though the boom is not essential for float legering it makes sense to use it for ease of change between the two methods. Then if I decide to change back to the float paternoster it is there ready. On the lead link end I have a snap link so I can easily add or remove the link. On the trace end I use another better quality snap link (a Berkley Cross lock). One modification I do make is to reinforce all the stress points with araldite instant metal. (See diagram).

JOHN ROBERT BAIT SAVERS

These little red plastic devices are very handy as they serve a number of purposes. Firstly they are highly visual which cannot to my mind detract from the pike attracting qualities of the bait. They also help me to find out which hook has the barb, when tackling up at first light. They also help to prevent the more fragile or clever baits from getting off the hook. I simply slip one over each barbed hook as I make up a trace. Traces with these bait savers are used for both live and deadbaits.

POP UPS

Sometimes there is an advantage to be had from popping up a dead or a livebait. Bottom weed can obscure a bait and certainly livebaits are rendered ineffective where there is a 6 to 12 inches of blanket weed. For livebaits I attach a Masterline mini egg which has

John Roberts bait savers, added attraction and a guide to which hook is barbed in the dark

Various ways of popping up deadbaits including Fox bait poppers, foam and balsa inserts

a ring with which I can wire the buoyancy aid to the eye of the treble. I can do the same with deadbaits or I can use one of two other methods.

Firstly I can simply inject air into a bait. This only works with fairly tough whole deadbaits such as smelt. I feel it also tends to push any juices in the bait out into the water. Secondly I use a Masterline balsa stick inserted into the deadbait. A piece of wire attaches the stick to the first treble thus avoiding the pike swallowing anything it should not. I am not keen on any forms of plastic foam or polystyrene inserts because they are almost certainly indigestible and though there is only a slight chance of a pike swallowing a bait popped up in this manner I'd rather not have to worry about it. Any extra means of popping a bait up should be attached to the trace so that it is always recovered.

One type of deadbait the pollan nearly always has the swim bladder intact and because of this it pops up without having to do anything to it at all. Generally pollan sold in bulk will always pop up. Those that are vacuum packed fresh may because of the packing process have the swim bladder crushed and will therefore sink like most other baits.

POLE ELASTIC

Though this is not immediately associated with pike fishing I have found one use for it. When bottom bouncing a live or deadbait one of the biggest problems is getting the lead snagged. By using a 12 inch link of size 14 pole elastic (a strong pole elastic for those who know nothing about such things). With a Drennan clip bead attached for the lead and a loop at the other end for attachment to my John Roberts Paternoster boom I then have a lead link that bounces out of most of the snags.

ROD RESTS

I've always used Gardner True Locks. These are light, very easy to adjust and they go into gravel quite easily, because of their fine points. I use True Lock back rod rest heads for the back rests. For drifter fishing I use the Gardner storm pole with a home made tube rod holder into which fits the rod. An angle lock allows the angle of the rod to be changed. The idea of this rod rest is to get the rod as high as possible thus allowing as much line to be pushed out by the wind. The storm pole extends to about 7 feet.

LANDING NET

My landing net is a standard 42 inch Gardner net to which is attached a two piece handle. The handle is 6 foot in total, but with one section removed gives me a 3ft handle for boat fishing. The handle is plugged with Duplon so that should I lose the lot overboard it floats. The very ends of the arms of the net are filled with Isopon and this is why the same net has lasted me 20 years. (Obviously the mesh had been replaced several times.) An additional modification is some petrol pipe tubing over the end of the arms. This prevents the arms wearing through the mesh. Cable ties hold the mesh in place top and bottom of the arm.

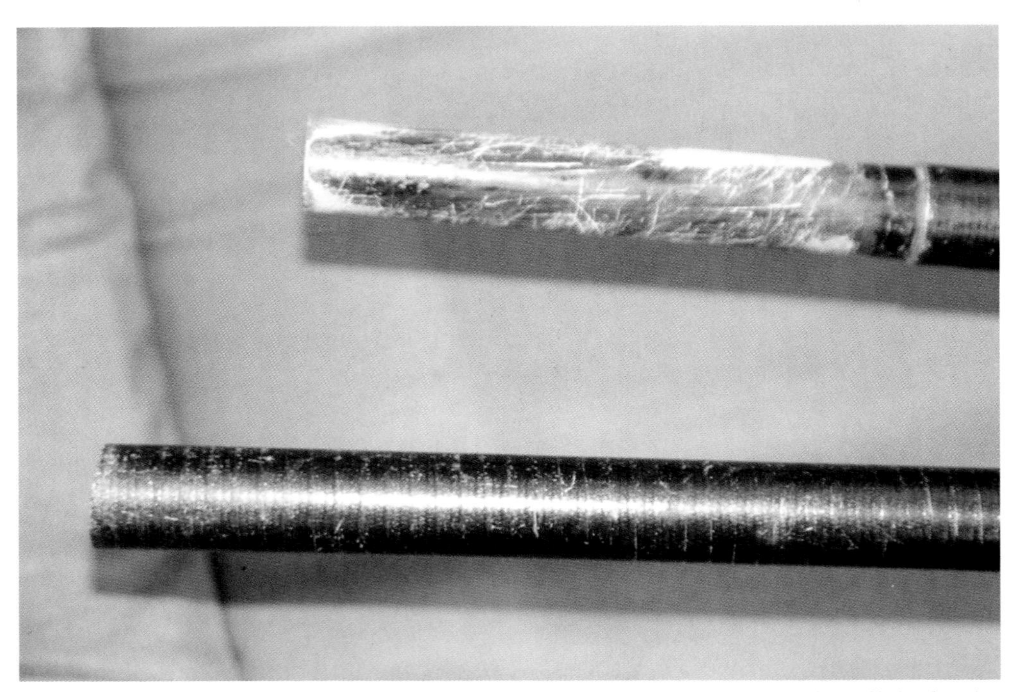

Home made extending landing net pole. Short for boat fishing, long for off the bank

For lure fishing I have a round 32 inch Masterline net which though pike friendly is a prone to getting lures snagged in it. I hope to get Masterline to change this for a knotless stiff netting which will still be pike friendly, but also resistant to lures.

Masterline Boat Net

LUGGAGE

My first piece of angling luggage was a huge six legged wicker basket that I could hardly carry. Luckily things have improved since then.

I like to keep my rods all neatly together. I have A Kevin Nash Super quiver into which I have fitted five 18 inch sections of Drennan triangular tube. These protect the tips and the butts of the rods. The floats are also protected as are the traces. The quiver also holds all my bank sticks and my landing net and brolly. The strap is heavily padded and when carried over the shoulder does not slip so that the quiver ends up horizontal. I have used the quiver for ten years and I've taken the precaution of keeping two more at present unused just in case they are changed in some way.

My modified holdall - note gaffer tape covered triangular tubes

To carry the rest of my fishing tackle I have either a Nash Pursuit 60 Rucksack for bank fishing or a Riva plastic box for boat fishing. In the rucksack or the box I have a Plano Magnum lure box which carries all my rig bits, floats, drop offs and so on. I have a 60lb set of Reuben Heaton Scales, an ET zip pike tube and an ET weigh sling. I also carry one of the old ET unhooking mats. Also carried are two rig bins covered in giant shrink tube to stop them cracking. My 35mm camera is carried in a professional foam filled camera case. This also includes a mini tripod and electronic cable release. I can also carry basic

My rucksack

cooking equipment such as a Coleman stove. A Petzel headlamp is always carried. If I am really struggling to get down the bank I also have a Fox two wheel barrow.

BIVVIES AND BROLLEYS

My bivvy is a Fox five rib Easydome. Its advantage to me is that it is very quick to erect and put away. For my fishing I do not need a home from home, just somewhere to spend a night and stay dry. My brolly is a 60 inch Fox Oval Brolly with a modified pole. I've replaced the aluminium pole with a fibre glass pole to save weight. I can screw an extra 2 foot long pole onto the end of it and in this way I can use it as a porch for the back of my vehicle.

CHAIRS AND BEDCHAIRS

I have had the same JRC recliner chair for fifteen years, such is the quality of modern chairs. A Fox bedchair is used for sleeping when I'm away from home, usually in the back of my vehicle.

CHEST WADERS FOOTWEAR AND CLOTHING

It does not matter how much fishing tackle you have and how much time you have to use it, you'll not survive long in winter on a fen drain or in a boat in the rain without good quality clothing. It is common knowledge that a number of thin layers is more effective than a few thick ones. Next to my skin I wear a Sundridge Sleepskin shirt. For trousers I have always favoured moleskin trousers. I find them to be warmer than jeans.

A Barometer is useful to predict changes in the weather

Next comes a Halkon Hunt wind stopper fleece. I usually also wear a wax proof waistcoat. The final layer is a Gore-Tex waterproof. You only have to look at what people who deal with extreme sports or exploration wear and it will be clear that Gortex is essential. Leggings are what let down most peoples waterproofing. I've tried everything over the years and the water always seems to find a way through. The problem with leggings is that you frequently end up sitting in a pool of water particularly when boat fishing. In this situation it is hardly suprising the water finds a way through. At the moment I am trying a bib and brace made by Touchstone. This has rubberised sections in the key areas. So far I've yet to have a wet bottom. Unfortunately that company is no longer in existence, but Masterline are going to try and produce a similar product.

I wear Derriboots in Field Boots where I need to walk and the paddling is limited. The normal Derriboots are worn when I need a totally waterproof boot. Chest waders are neoprenes and these are useful in swims where you cannot get a bait in the water without wading, for example where there are extensive reedbeds such as in Ireland in April and May.

MICROCAT BAIT BOAT

The Microcat is one of the most sophisticated bait boats available. It is made by a company called Angling Technics. I have had one for the past 13 years and I couldn't do without it. Firstly let me explain how it works and what it is capable of. It has a twin hull construction which means that it is quite a big boat. This is essential if you going to use it on a large water. It is powered by pumps rather than propellers and this largely eliminates problems with weed. It also solves the problem of the line fouling the propeller. It is controlled by a standard radio controlled model handset with rechargeable batteries. These will last several days depending on use. The boat itself is powered by two batteries and again in normal use you can expect a couple of days between charging. Both the handset and the boat can be recharged from a car lighter socket or a solar panel. I carry a set of spare batteries because the Microcat is one of the few baitboats that you can easily change the batteries.

My particular Microcat has the added digital echo sounder which simply shows the depth. You can get a graphical display which is useful if you want to have a better idea of what the bottom is like or whether there is weed present. I find the echo sounder to be essential on waters where the depth is very variable. It is no good dropping your bait off in the only part of a lake or reservoir that is 1ft deep. (Unless the pike happen to be there).

Needless to say I have made some limited modifications to my boat. All baits are carried in one of the twin compartments. Each compartment can be released individually. All works well when using deadbaits or prebait, however livebaits present certain problems. Simply a livebait can jump out of the compartment. I solve this problem with a plastic cover for the bait compartment and this is held in place with

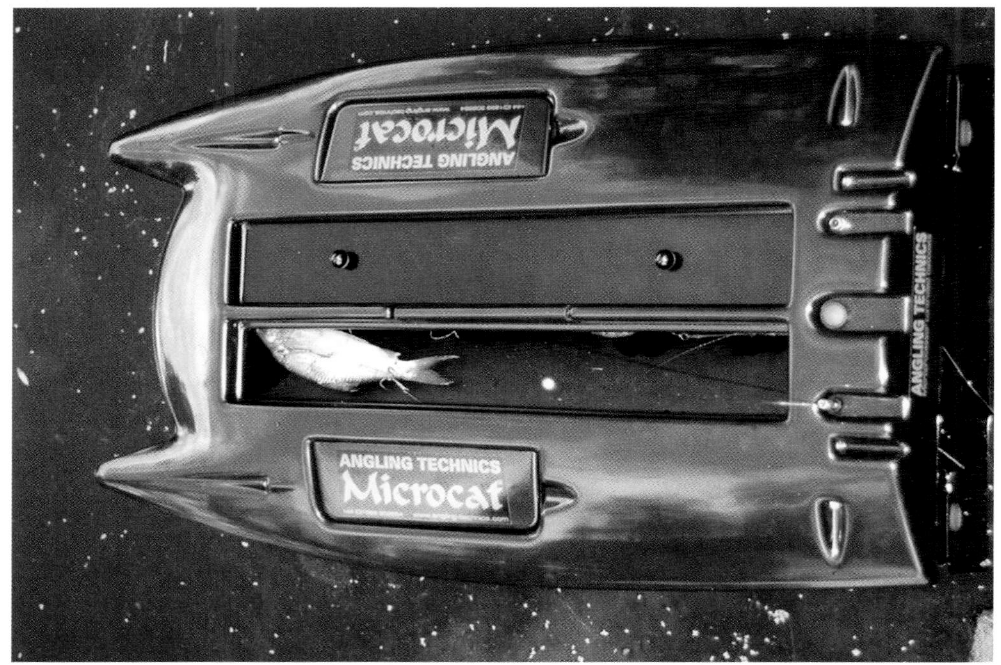

Micro Bait Boat, my best friends when it comes to putting baits where the pike are. (before holes and battery boxes were taped up)

Velcro. As the bait is taken out by the boat it is refreshed by the water which flows through the compartment. I usually tape up all the battery compartments and in this way very little water is shipped even during a long journey on a windy day.

As an additional aid a standard feature of the Microcat is a set of direction lights. These are very useful in the dark and in poor light conditions at extreme range. If your eyesight is poor and you are over 200 yards out binoculars are useful. You can also get a Maglight attachment so that you can see really well at long range in the dark. Its maximum range is around 250 yards which allows you to reach areas which cannot normally be fished such as overhanging trees. Livebaits can be hooked very lightly and they are not stunned by casting.

When loading up I always put the lead in the right hand compartment and the bait in the left hand one. By doing this I avoid tangles on dropping the bait off. Just before dropping the bait I put the reel into Baitrunner mode and close the bale arm. This tightens everything up. I also keep the rod tip sunk in order to drag the braid under the surface. I know this sounds crazy, but I also think the sound of the boat can stir the pike up. I have certainly had takes as soon as the bait is released. I remember demonstrating this several times to Des Taylor on Stamford Reservoir years ago.

It should also be realised that a bait boat is not just for static baits. You can drop a free roving livebait out as well as a drifter. This is particularly useful with a drifter when you have 30 yards of flat calm water in front of you.

Neville Fickling waits in hope on a Yorkshire Pit

SPECIALISED EQUIPMENT

In this category I'm going to deal with equipment that most people either do not have or do not bother with. Most people would not dream of putting a freezer in the back of their car for a trip away. Yet so many places I have stayed when on a fishing holiday do not have freezer space. I solve this by taking a small upright freezer with me. At home I also have an upright freezer dedicated to my supply of deadbaits.

Chucking a modest(?) livebait out

Livebaits are probably the most important bait I use. Because of this great care is taken to source the right baits and keep them alive. I have two one hundred gallon tanks connected together by two inch waste pipe. One of these is connected to a wheelie bin which serves as a settling tank. Two foot off of the bottom of the bin is the water recirculation pump. This draws water and runs into a gravel filter made from an old Daiwa box. Three two inch waste pipes go into one pipe before going back to the first livebait tank in the chain. This means that there are about 250 gallons of water in circulation. Two separate aerators go into each tank. On the bottom of the wheelie bin is a drain off pipe to remove the waste material. A hose pipe from the outside tap goes to the first tank and once a week I top up with fresh water. In the first tank I will have up to 150 trout. In the second tank I will have up to 150 coarse fish. In the wheelie bin I keep my jack pike livebaits. Once every two weeks I add some anti fungal agent into the system.

Part of my livebait system - the two big tanks contain different types of bait

A good supply of bait is essential

Before I go on a trip it is obviously time consuming trying to catch the baits before I go, therefore I select my baits and keep them in a smaller tank in the garage. A flood-light over the main tank system allows me to see what I am doing. All the tanks have lids to keep the baits in and the debris out. A square landing net makes catching baits much easier.

An earlier version of my livebait storage system, now the retaining tanks are bigger

BOAT FISHING

For good or bad I must have an unbeaten record of boat and engine ownership in the UK. I sat down before writing this and counted the number of boats I had owned. Even I was horrified when it came to a total of 18. The engine score is not a lot better a total of 15 without counting electrics. The list of boats I have used is as follows and understandably I do not own them all now.

9 ft fibre glass
13 ft 6 inch fibre glass
14 ft Orkney Clinker Built (mahogany!)
Five different fibre glass boats.
Three Tarbour Yaks.
A 15 ft 10 inch Bonwitcho With
A 11ft Bonwitcho With
A 14 ft 6 inch Demonstrator

My small boat - where I cannot get the big boat in. A Water Tender

A 10 ft Sniper.
A 9ft 4 inch Water Tender.
A 7ft Tarbour Yak.
An 11 ft Dory.
A 17 ft 6 inch Wilson Flyer.

The engines were.
A 1.5hp Seagull
A 4hp Seagull
Two 4hp Johnson's.
A 4hp Mariner
A 6hp Johnson.

Two 9.8hp Mercury's.
A 15hp Mariner.
A 10hp Selva.
Two 30hp Mariners one short, one longshaft.
A 70hp Johnson.
A 50hp Yamaha.
A 5hp Mercury.

The electric motor score runs to 4 including a 30lb thrust Shakespeare when they first came out. Then a 38lb thrust Shakespeare, a 3hp Minn Kota and finally a 50lb thrust Minn Kota.

With this wealth of boat and engine owning experience I feel that I am well able to give practical advice on boat fishing. Why then does a serious pike angler need a boat? Well, unless you can walk on water restricting yourself to bank fishing only will see a large variety of pike waters closed to effective angling. So many of our best waters are big lakes, Lochs and Loughs. Even our biggest rivers are extremely difficult to fish without the aid of a boat. Go to the Norfolk Broads and you will be lost without a boat.

Most pike angler's first experience with a boat will be when they fish a special event such as on one of our trout reservoirs. Or they will hire a boat when having a break on somewhere like the Norfolk Broads. It is even possible that you will have a day's guided pike fishing somewhere in the UK. You can do this on the Broads, The Lake District and I myself do a limited amount on my local waters such the River Severn and also on Windermere.

Hire boats come in all shapes and sizes. They range from fairly new good quality boats to very old tubs that would in some cases be better off filled with compost and used as a flower display. As a prospective boat angler you should always be prepared for the worst. If you are lucky the boat will come with an engine. If not your initiation requires you to learn to row. It is suprising how many pike anglers have never performed this simple task. The time to learn and it a simple thing, is not on a big water with a strong wind. Even if you have to gain practical experience on your local boating lake it is a good idea and you'll also keep the wife and kids amused.

Gary Banks with a Derravaragh 27-08

How then do you row? Well the key thing is to try and keep the blades vertical and if they are curved use them with the curve pushing into the water. Short shallow strokes are more effective than long deep strokes which see half the oar disappear under the water. Depending on what sort of rowlock you have this will also see the oar jumping out of the rowlock. This in nautical terms is known as "catching a crab" Some rowlocks have a bar over the top which prevents this and even better, thole pins mean that you cannot easily lose an oar when you stop rowing... With oars using rowlocks you should have the plastic collar pressed right up to the rowlock. This gives you maximum leverage and also protects the oars from wear. A good rowing boat will have a footboard so you can brace your feet against it and row more easily.

The secret of going in the direction you want to is to row with different strokes on one side to turn in the opposite direction. To reverse, just do the rowing in the reverse direction. To turn 180 degrees simply row forward on one oar and reverse on the other. It sounds difficult, but infact it's probably easier that learning to ride a bike.

The maximum distance a fit person can row on a reasonably calm day non stop is probably about 1 to 2 miles. In the old days in Ireland before the advent of the outboard motor the Victorian pike fisherman visiting Lough Mask would have a couple of boatmen cum ghillies with him. They must have been very hardy in those days.

Sooner or later everyone comes face to face with an outboard motor. All are different even those made by the same manufacturer in the same year. What you realise is that the person hiring the engine will invariably know his own engines little foibles so listen carefully to what he has to say. All hire engines will have a choke and they will also have a starting position on the throttle. Assuming that our boat hirer is half competent you will have a full fuel tank and the fuel switch if present will be on. The air vent screw on top of the petrol tank will also be open. All you have do then is pull the starter cord. It is usually a good idea to hold on to the top of the engine as you pull. Where the engine has a gearbox, make sure it is out of gear. If you have a boat companion and you are on the engine you should be in charge. Make sure he is sitting down and not looking over your shoulder. I nearly laid Gary Banks out one day giving one particular engine an extra hard pull. Most engines should start after two or three pulls at the most. If it doesn't start vary the throttle and choke setting slightly and usually it will fire. Some engine can have the choke switched off straight away; others need 30 seconds to warm up. Make sure you do close the choke otherwise the engine will only manage about half speed if that. A simple check you should always make is to ensure that cooling water is coming out from below the engine.

To set out with an engine without a gearbox, you'll usually have to reverse by rotating the whole engine. Most engines do have gearboxes with a forward neutral and reverse. Always change gear while the engine is ticking over. Crashing the gear at high revs it is going to make the owner shout at you and when the gearbox fails you may be miles from home. Outboards are designed happily to run at full throttle so that is the setting most of use to get from A to B. There are not many things that can go wrong, but the commonest is a loss of power with vibration which is usually due to weed fouling the propeller. Simply reverse the direction of thrust and this usually clears the weed. If the engine stops dead with a clunk it is usually because of something much stronger than weed fouling the prop. In 2003 on Ladybower when waters were very low there were a lot of anchor ropes floating near the surface. Now at normal water levels these would be 40 foot down. These had been lost by trout anglers who had not tied the anchor rope to the boat! Neville Fickling and I were racing along to one of our favourite spots when suddenly the engine expired and we were stopped like an aircraft on an arrester cable. It took about 15 minutes cutting with a rather blunt knife to dispose of the offending rope. A total loss of propulsion just after you hit something with the engine will normally be a shear pin or spring. You can tell for sure because the engine revs, but you go nowhere. Replacing a shear pin or spring is quite simple if you know what you are doing. First though you must have a spare shear pin. These have an uncanny knack of dropping out of your hand into 20 feet of inky water so be careful. Usually a spare will be located under the cowling in a rubber mounting block. To change the pin on something like a Mariner 4hp, remove the split pin from the nut holding the propeller on. This unscrews and then you can remove the propeller. As you do this the broken shear pin will generally drop out. Put the new one in its slot replace the propeller and then the nut which should have the split pin hole aligned with the shaft hole. Do not over tighten. Generally it is best to use a new split pin, but if you have no choice reuse the old one. All of this is more easily carried out on the bank with the engine tilted.

Most engines have a shallow tilt option; this can save you a lot of broken shear pins. Bigger engines employ devices such as splined hubs which prevent damage to the gear shaft if you hit a rock. Hire engines are often abused by incompetent customers and some hirers sensibly make you pay a deposit to cover damage to parts such as the propeller. If in doubt, particularly if you can see the bottom put the engine in neutral and row.

Very few people understand the performance characteristics of their outboard motors. In order to get the best out of your engine you really need to know what the optimum settings are for your engine. Typically I've experimented and ended up using the wrong propeller. All that happened was that I didn't go as fast and I used more fuel. By setting the pitch of the propeller correctly you can reduce the engine rpm for any given speed. In so doing you save fuel or go faster depending on your requirement.

Having got to wherever you need to go you will by now be looking at the bow anchor and rope that comes with the boat. The anchor will probably be a pathetically small effort which wouldn't hold you out in a breeze. There will probably not be enough rope either. If you do decide to anchor and cannot then your days fishing is already ruined. I will deal in detail with anchors when I talk about my ideal boat fishing set up. A hire boat never has a stern anchor so you should always take something with you. Something good and solid weighing around 20 to 30lb will do the job. Do not be tempted to use 56lb weights as they will cripple you when lifting out of 25 feet of water.

Plenty of cleats distributed around the boat for mooring ropes and back anchors - you can also use a cleat to hold a landing net with a pike inside

of resin in all and a hundred foot of matting. Under the engine well I built a drainage sump which doubles as a livebait well.

Next two knees on each side which support the gunwhale and strengthen the side of the boat. The cuddy entrance and door were constructed along with small bunks made from ply and glass fibre again. These are used for storage. Finally the bulkhead that holds the foredeck up was made from ply again and glassed in. I cut out a rectangle on the front of the foredeck and constructed an anchor box. Now I had to start attaching the bits and pieces. Instead of pedestal type seats I have opted for a couple of fibre glass boxes with swivel seats. These boxes are used for extra fuel, fenders, rod rests and a 12V battery. A set of stainless steel bow rails make lifting the anchor much safer. A bow roller for pulling and lowering the anchor without wearing part of the boat is fitted. Three rope cleats, two on the foredeck one on the cuddy roof and a rope guide help keep the anchor rope pointing the way it is meant to be. On the transom I fitted an auxiliary engine bracket and a stainless steel engine plate. Two cleats one on each side for the rear anchor. Two rope guides plus a roller for lifting the rear anchor.

Next I fitted the engine remote steering and throttle control, echo sounder bracket and transducer. The two 25 litre fuel tanks fit below the engine well at the back and a set of oars sit in big Terry clips below the gunwhale. Inside the cuddy is a cigarette lighter socket so that I can plug my GPS or phone into charge. Six Berkley type rod rests are flush mounted, three on each side. The floor area is kept clear of all tackle and has a non slip surface covered with carpet and an unhooking matt when a fish is landed. Just a tip for those trying to save a bob or two. You can make a good non slip floor by painting and then sprinkling a coating of sand over the wet paint.

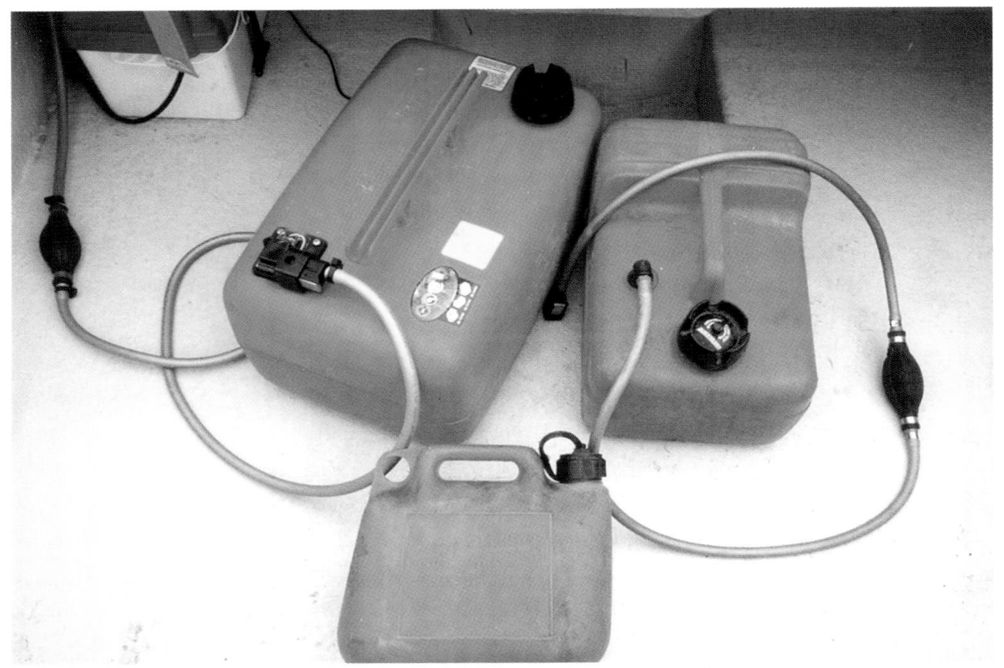

Take plenty of fuel! I always keep a gallon can as my last resort reserve

Though I had previously used a second hand Johnson 70hp 2 stroke on this boat and reached 44mph the Johnson was too expensive to run and anyway I blew it up! I replaced it with the current engine a 50hp Yamaha four stroke and this uses less than half of the Johnson's 7 gallons an hour. Also there is no oil to worry about. It gives the boat a maximum speed of 33mph fully loaded. The engine itself is 3 cylinders, 3 carburettors and an overhead cam. It has power trim and tilt which when used gives you better fuel economy and speed. At low speed to going onto plane the trim is full down and once on the plane you trim up to get optimum performance. I always carry two separate fuel tanks with their own fuel lines plus a spare can with 12 litres for the 5hp Mercury back up engine which also fits the big engine in an absolute emergency.

In the spares box is a spare propeller, three brand new spark plugs. A spare fuse for the Yamaha. A plug spanner and a blade and posidrive screwdriver. An adjustable spanner, a metre long piece of plastic coated wire, some cable ties large and small, a towel and a spare fuel pipe connector for each engine. Also included are two flares, a spare bung and insulation tape. All are carried in an air tight bucket along with a can of WD40. Two life jackets are stored and 30 foot of rope with a float attached should my boat companion jump over the side and then decide he doesn't want to end it all. A baler is essential and these are easily made out of the handle half of a 5 litre plastic container.

Testing the enging in a water tank. Check the cooling water is coming out as a distinct and powerful jet

The Wilson Flyer on the plane

VHF Radio + GPS for keeping in touch

Twin axle trailer

Most boat insurance policies specify a fire extinguisher which has to be of a powder type because a petrol fire is the most likely source of combustion.

For nearly all boat fishing you will need an echo sounder. I have a bracket on the Wilson Flyer to which I attach my sounder and the transducer is permanently mounted on the stern. The same sounder can be used with a portable kit when I'm using a hire boat or one my smaller craft. At the moment my sounder is just a fairly basic model Eagle, but if I get around to it I'll fit a combined GPS plotter and sonar. These days the sophistication of GPS plotters is mind boggling. You can actually have a rolling display map of where you are fishing. All the safe routes from A to B can be plotted onto this chart; all you have to do is follow the plotted course. With this sort of equipment you are as safe as you ever can be travelling at speed. You also have the advantage of being able to make journeys in the dark and fog remembering however that this is not radar and you still have to take due care that someone else is not out there. A compass is always carried, but do remember the deviation from true North to magnetic North. An O/S map will enable you to compensate if you have a compass to guide you.

To get the boat to where you are fishing you need a trailer. Now while a small boat can be carried using a lightweight trailer towed behind your average car or van, once you get to big boats the trailer has to be substantial and the vehicle larger too. Most Four Wheel Drives and Transits sized vans are rated to tow 750kg. Above this weight your trailer has to be braked. My trailer was built by myself after having a quote of £1300.

Twin axles are a good idea for a heavy boat - don't forget to take two spare wheels though

So I went to a scrap yard and got four mini wheels and fitted new tyres. I then bought a trailer stub axle and four of the heaviest they did (500kg per wheel). Then I bought the steel, drilled it and welded it before having it all galvanised. I fitted 11 centre rollers and six outside posts with double rollers on the top. A two speed 1500kg winch enables me to winch the boat on the trailer with one hand. The wheel bearings are always greased before I go anywhere and I use high speed waterproof grease. An ordinary trailer is only rated at 50mph and rated at 60psi. Mini wheels are rated at 80mph and only need 28psi. A four wheel trailer is a lot better for your boat than a two wheel one. If I go further than 50 miles I always take two spare tyres. As a safety measure on my towing hitch there is a piece of ten ton hawser cable. The towing ball needs to be greased before you set out otherwise you will wear the towing hitch. When you are carrying your engine mounted on the back of the boat you need to have a propeller cover. To avoid straining the engine mounting a piece of 2 by 2 under the engine saddle supports it in the tilted position.

The whole shebang is strapped down using a lorry ratchet strap near the transom where there's plenty of strength in the boat. The other strap goes across the bows in front of the cuddy. I never strap across the middle of the boat because this is the weaker point of the boat and the pressure of a strap could damage it. The trailer board is attached using elastic straps and the cable is strapped to the winch post in order to avoid dragging on the floor.

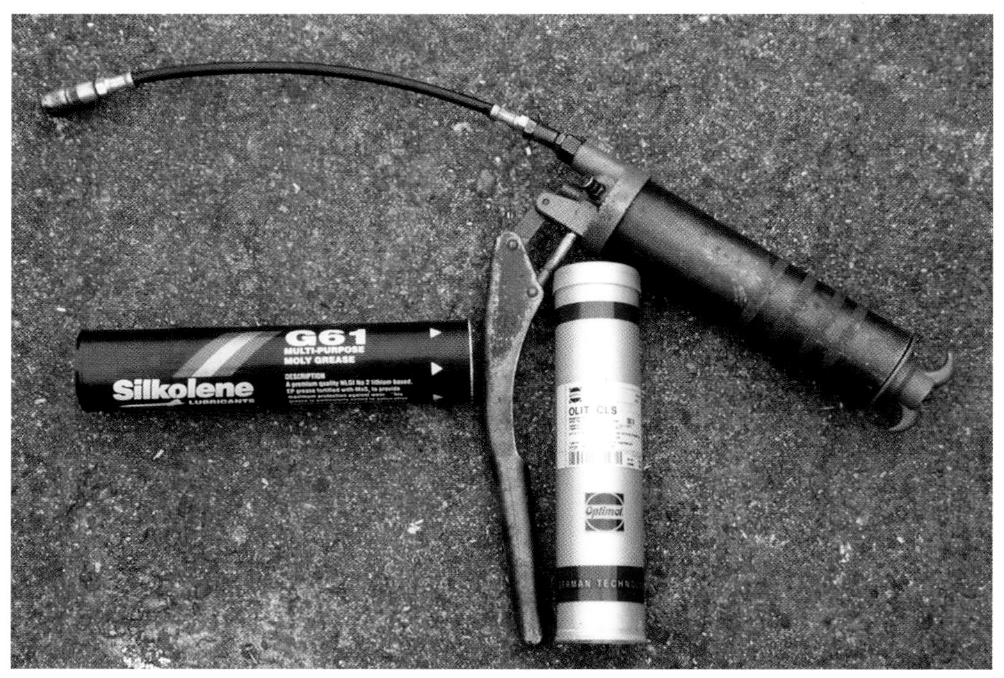

Wheel bearings need greasing regularly with high quality grease - a grease gun is essential

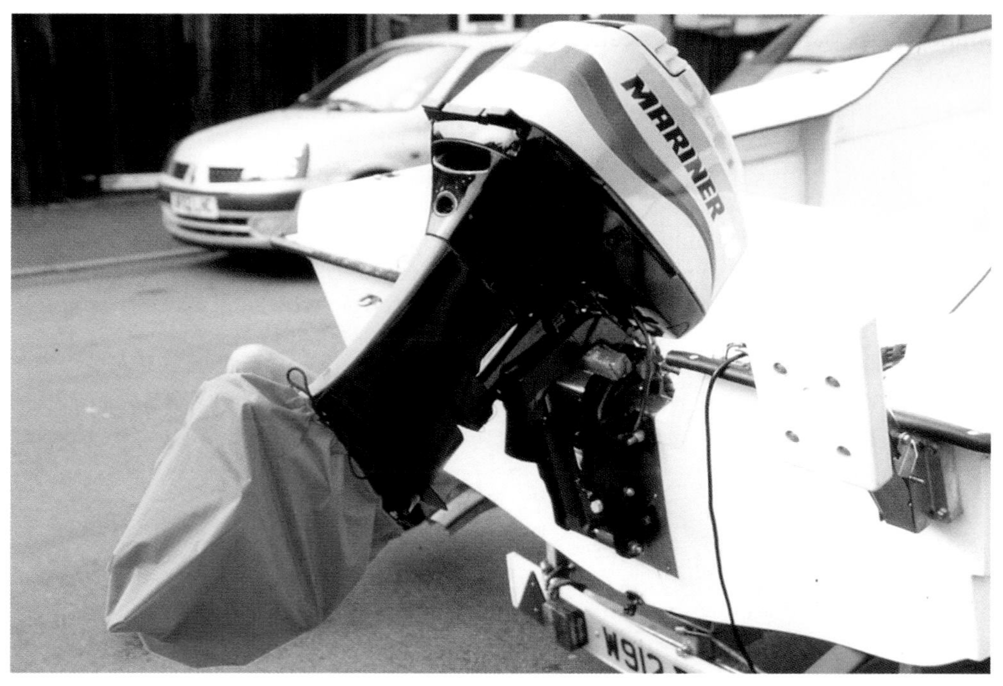

Outboard motor prop cover. Where you do not have a power tilt to kee the engine up a hammer handle or suitable piece of wood needs to be used to support the engine

Generally when launching any boat from a slipway it is far easier to load all the tackle before you launch. The same applies in reverse. Always put the bung in and have a short painter to hold onto when you float off the trailer otherwise you could say goodbye to your boat as one well known Loch fishing legend once did on Esthwaite. I mention no names here, but his name is similar to a well known high street menswear chain.

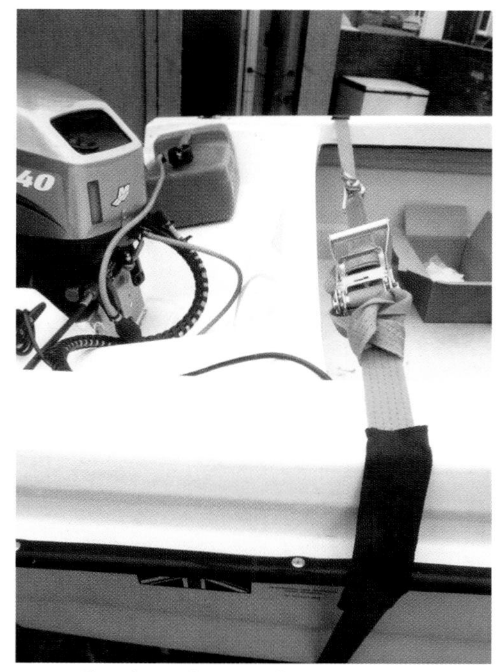

Good quality ratchet straps are essential when towing a boat

Once out on the water we come to anchoring. The Wilson flyer though a big boat is generally no less of a problem than a Lough boat to anchor. What it does suffer from is wave slap. It can be very noisy with waves slapping the front of the boat. As a rule I always try to fish a little further away from the boat in shallow water. The anchor I use is a tried and tested hand made design made by Gary Banks. At present there is a Mark 1 and a Mark 2 version. The original Mark 1 has four round cross section prongs and a weighed shank. This in turn has another iron bar joined to it by a chain. An extra iron bar can be added for extra grip, but remember you have to lift this sometimes out of deep water. The prongs dig into the bed and the extra bar lifts up and down with the wave motion without shifting the anchor. The Mark 2 has more flattened prongs which gives better grip in softer material.

My anchor rope is made of climbing rope and though expensive lasts forever. The best place to get such a rope cheap is off a climber because they regularly replace their ropes. To the end of this I have a polystyrene net float so that if for any reason I lose the anchor it doesn't sink without trace. I nearly managed this with someone's anchor on Rutland Water when my knot came undone. Luckily I was able to snag the rope and make good the loss. To the end of the rope I have a D shackle which I tie on and whip with braid so it can never come off. I cover that with insulation tape. The shackle is so I can attach an extra bar if the weather is rough. As a rule you need 3 times the depth of water in rope paid out to enable the anchor to hold on a windy day. For a rear anchor I use a relatively light weight which I can pull quickly if there are problems with a frisky fish. It consists of about 15 inches of 4 inch stainless tube filled with lead. This dives down into the mud adding to its grip. An eye bolt is cast into the lead of the weight and to this attached a quick release clip which attaches to the rope, again with a polystyrene float. If a pike should get around the back anchor, I open the bale arm and make sure it is free running. Then I lift the back anchor very slowly completely into the boat and then unclip the weight. Keeping the braid slack to the fish I then untangle the line from the rope.

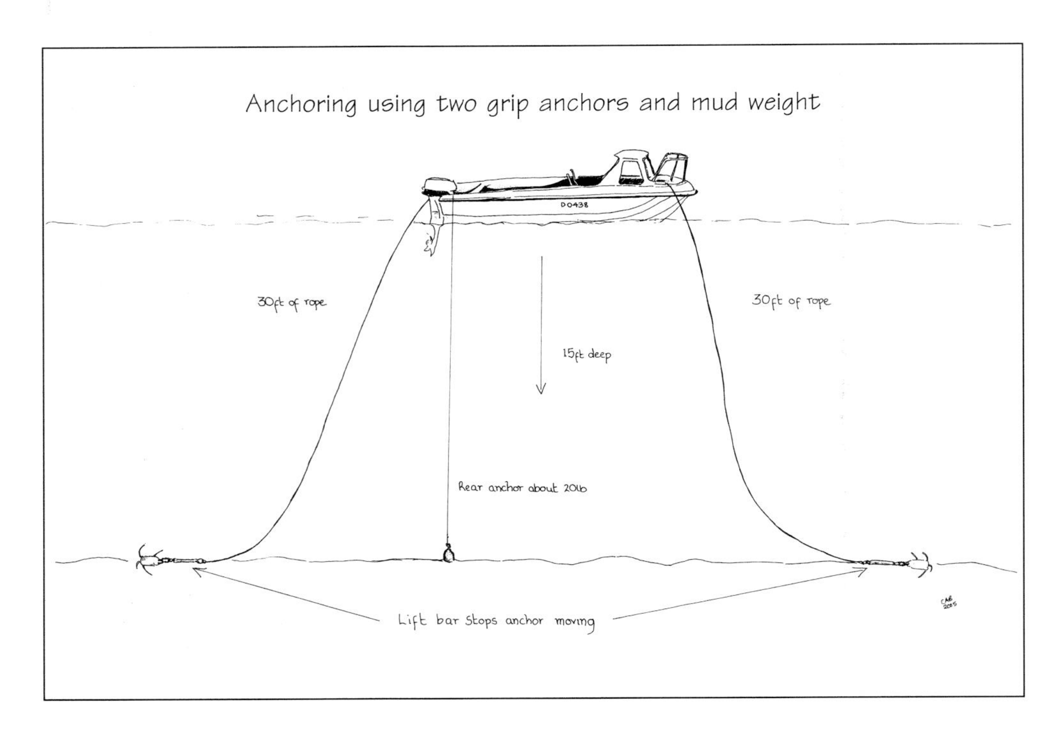

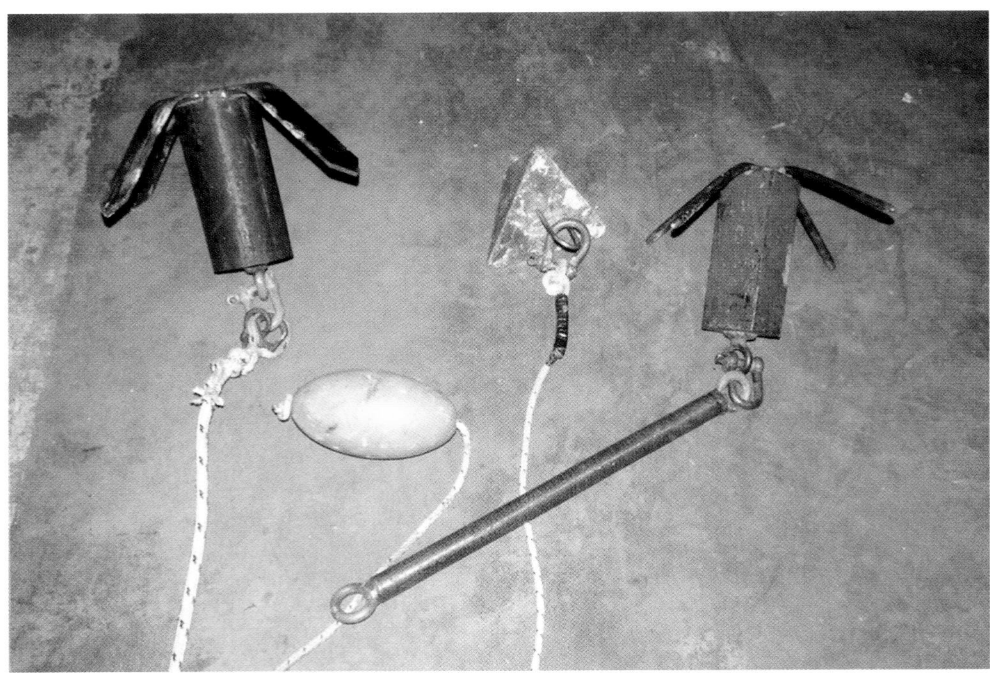

Front and back anchors. Left: Mark 2 front anchor with wider tines for better grip. Middle, lead pyramid back anchor. Right: Mark 1 front anchor with long bar to enable anchor grip.

When anchoring I follow this procedure. I find the swim; let's say it is 18 feet deep. I let the front anchor go down and release another 20 feet of rope. The rope is attached to the cleat. As long as there is enough wind the boat will settle at the end of the rope. While I am setting up it gives the anchor chance to grip and then this avoids the problem of casting out all your rods and finding out you are drifting. Next I drop the back anchor and let out a foot of extra rope to allow for my movement in the boat. I then go back to the front anchor rope and pull until the boat stops swinging and retie to the cleat. It is also possible to anchor using two grip anchors, I have shown how to do this in the diagram.

Two little tips about anchors and small boats. Never trailer the boat with anchors in the bottom of the boat and always keep your rods on the opposite side to where the anchor is. Anchors are heavy and it is not unknown for someone to drop one. Pulling it into the boat next to your rods is asking for trouble. It is good practice where possible to store the anchor and rope in a small crate or box, but on my big boat there is a box on the bow for the front anchor and the back anchor sits in the engine well.

On hire boats I use this type of clamp onto which I have pop riveted a Roberts type boat rest. On my own boat they are permanently mounted

Safety always has to be a prime consideration when boat fishing. Someone quite wisely said that no fish is worth a life. In the UK there have been two tragedies associated with boats, one was Andy Munday on Queenford lagoon the other was Keith Sellick on Savay. Neither were on particular big waters. In the United Kingdom and Ireland a number of people have died on big waters such as Loch Awe. Usually because people have not followed basic rules. For example 4 anglers went out on Loch Awe in a 14 foot boat. Now if they were big people a boat that size would be quite heavily loaded and it only takes one mistake to change a fun day out into a disaster.

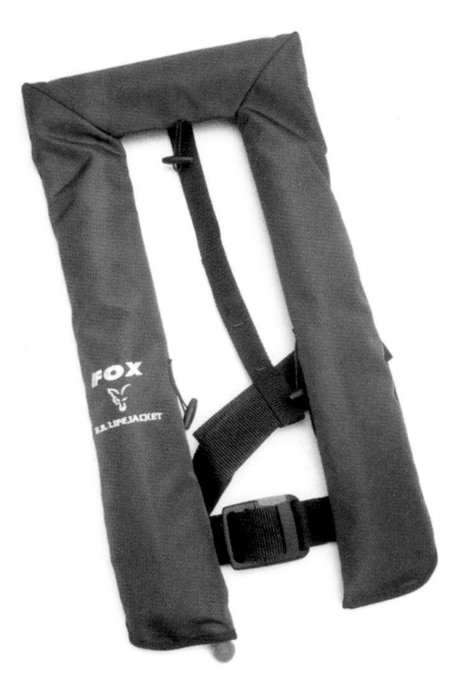

Whenever conditions are extreme or when I'm climbing up on the front of the boat I wear a Fox life jacket

As I write this I have just returned from a trip to Sweden. Included during the week were 3 days fishing at Vastervick on the Baltic. While we were there the weather was variable, but on the third day it was quite windy. There were two other pike anglers present and they quite sensibly kept to more sheltered water. Neville Fickling and I on the other hand wanted to go much further afield. The boats in use were sturdy 15 footers with 15hp engines, but not what both of us had been used to recently. We got out to one area and then moved having caught three small pike. On the way back there were sections which were quite rough, but nothing that boat could not handle. We had travelled within the limitations of the weather. If we had gone to where we wanted to go and took a chance we would have got there and returned. However the battering we would have had and the occasional thought that we shouldn't have been there would not have been very entertaining. So we probably missed out on some fish, but at no time were we at risk. The others did not go anywhere near as far because they were new to big water pike fishing. Both sets of anglers fished to their own limitations and everyone was fine. Where problems arise is when someone develops a gung ho attitude and starts to takes risks.

Certain basic precautions have to be taken. You must know where you are going and how to get back. You certainly cannot wander about without an echo sounder or a chart of the depths. You need ample fuel and these days a mobile phone is vital. If the weather deteriorates you should consider going to the bank near some habitation and either wait until the weather improves or walk or hitch home or phone for assistance. When you are hiring boats the owners will always prefer that you call for help rather than risk losing yourself and their boat. Though it is not always possible try and give someone an idea what the latest time will be when you intend to return.

Weather forecasts are available throughout the day on radio and TV and in the UK and Ireland the BBC Radio 4 Shipping forecast will give you a good idea of the trends. Generally if the area you are fishing is surrounded by Force 7 or more forecasts then you are unlikely to get out on a big water. Then is the time to have some smaller back-up waters available. A lot also depends on the direction of the wind. On Loch Lomond for example you could still fish the West bank out of Arden in a force 6 from the West. You would find it difficult fishing on the Balmaha side in such conditions. A similar position prevailed on Blithfield a few years ago. The wind was so strong from the West that boats were only allowed to fish the West bank. John Davey had a 37 pounder and everyone returned in one piece.

If you do get caught out on a big open water try to keep going straight into the wind, but realise that you will ship water so some bailing will have to be done. Try and make use of any available shelter even it means going slightly out of your way. Avoid as much as possible going across a big swell, but whatever you do once you are committed to doing something keep going. The last thing you want to do is turn around or have an argument with a mate about it! If you should be so unlucky as to have an engine pack in, provided the water is not too deep use the front anchor to try and ride out the bad weather. If you consider the sizes of boats that some people have crossed the Atlantic in you should be able to cope with what the weather throws at you.

One of biggest problems for the man at the engine in a relatively slow boat is spray. Modern clothing will keep you dry, but constant buckets of water thrown in your face make it difficult to see which way you are going. You can usually predict when the next soaking is coming so I simply look sideways for a couple of seconds. Though you should have a life jacket it is no use pretending that it alone can save your life. Exposure times in water are such that survival is shorter the colder the water. Immersion suits are available these days from companies such as Sundridge and some pike anglers do wear these. However it is far better not to get into a life threatening situation from the start. If you can afford a big boat then you will be much better equipped to fish big waters. I've seen some hire boats on Lomond what are used for pike fishing and when fully loaded there appears to be about 6 inches of leeway between the gunwhales and the water. I'd rather be in debt forever than fish in boat like that again.

BAIT

DEADBAITS

When I was a kid I could get my mackerel myself from the sea and then later I'd go to Wolverhampton fish market. As kids we used to use a lot of sprats or "tin hats" as we used to call them. We would mount them for wobbling using a single treble on a trace attached via a snap link. The trace minus treble would be threaded using an old fashioned baiting needle though the mouth and then out through the flank. The hook was then reattached. It was ages before I had much confidence in herrings and mackerel as bait, but that has obviously changed since then.

Wherever you pike fish, unless you are restricted to artificials you are going to need a supply of dead or livebaits. Deadbaits are simple; you can buy them in bulk from Neville Fickling's Tackle Shop in Gainsborough. I'm lucky I get mine for nothing by endorsing his products. My favourite baits before Christmas are sardines and mackerel. Later in the season I like to use smelt and lamprey. I prefer to use the head end of lamprey because a couple of times I have had problems with tail sections. On one occasion on the North Level I had runs and missed them because the trebles had hooked up with each other. Tails seem to be particularly prone to this. One of the fish I lost might have been a really big fish. The same problem can arise using eel sections. I do like the head end of a pound eel and like the head end of a lamprey it gives out lots of blood and juices. Though there are lots of other baits available the four mentioned do for most of my pike fishing. I have one or two dodges that I like to use when deadbaiting. When a bait has been used for a while I like to stab it with a knife or squash it under foot. On big waters where I think a decent scent trail is important I'll take a mackerel or sardine and tear the head off with a pair of forceps, again to release the juices.

Flavourings are always worth a try, they certainly cannot do any harm

If the water has been given a hammering on the usual deadbaits I prefer a large natural dead such as a skimmer or a carp, preferably around the 8oz mark. These often pop up naturally so I avoid stabbing these. I also like freshly killed baits and I'll sometimes cut a flap of flesh off them to release more scent. Fresh baits have not had the cell structure destroyed by freezing and consequently do not seem to smell of much to me at least!

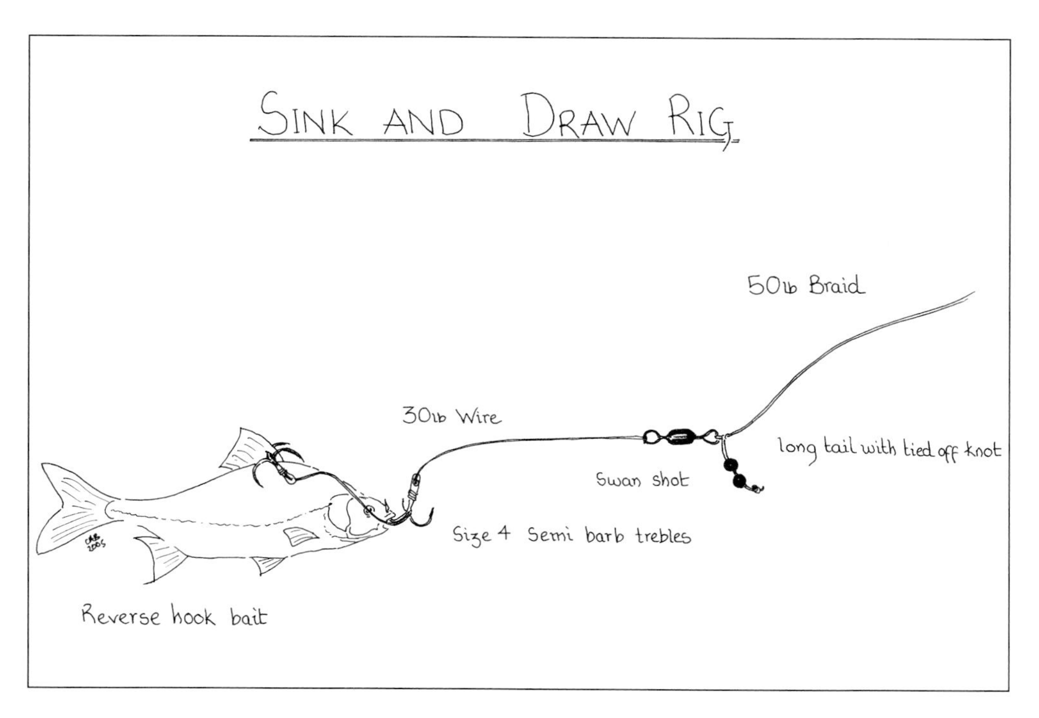

Flapper removed from mackerel bait to let out more scent

I did have a bit of success once with garfish and sandeels, particularly hair rigged and frozen already mounted for really hard casting. Bait boats have to some extent reduced the need to do this on most waters.

Other than the usual baits I'm a great fan of dead jack pike of 1 to 1½lb. These I catch myself from canals or small pits where there are lots of small pike. When using them on a couple of large trebles I often attach a stringer of 15lb line from the jaw of the pike to the top treble so that when a pike ejects the bait I get the bait back. Hitting a run requires the same tactics as for live jack pike. I wait a timed three minutes and in this way you hook the pike cleanly every time.

LIVEBAITS

Livebaits take a lot more effort to obtain and keep. When I was 11 or 12 I was already keeping livebaits in a tank at the bottom of my parent's garden. There was no aeration and I used to keep gudgeon caught from my local canal. I learned how to catch them in a bottle trap which I made from a brandy bottle. Using a glass cutter and a large screw driver the cone in the bottom of the bottle was knocked out. A few holes were punched into the cap and the whole thing was baited with bread and lowered into the water on a length of string.

I also had a Tupperware livebait cage. I purloined one of my mother's bread bins and made holes in it with a red hot poker. With a brick inside it the whole thing plus hapless gudgeon was sunken in the canal. These days I am better organised and this is dealt with in detail under specialised tackle.

LURES

Lures can be very effective at catching pike, but time and time again natural baits will beat the socks off of artificial lures. There are times however when lures are the only method available. Quite a few trout waters allow deadbaits and lures, but in reality only lures will offer any real prospect of success. You therefore have a choice, get up to naughty tricks and probably catch a big pike fairly quickly (and get banned) or learn to lure fish! On waters such as Blithfield anyone who fails to conform to the rules is likely to get lynched so on that water at least, if it was caught, it fell to a lure.

Like most pike anglers I started off with lure fishing, but from those early days it was a somewhat slow progression. My first pride and joy as a young lure angler was an ABU Killer plug. I remember fishing at Burlington Pool a water which had a walkway around part of it. The desire to reach those monster pike which were obviously out of reach of anything but a superhuman cast saw me project said lure into a tree. Imagine the misery and despair that this induced. All that stood between me and success with pike was that tree! I had no way of getting it back from where I stood, but luckily I managed to convince my parents to fetch my single seater canoe. Having obtained permission from the angling club I rescued that lure, but I don't think I ever caught much on it after that. All in all a waste of time.

Lures do this to people. You buy a particular model because you are convinced that this or that lure is going to catch the big one. Very few lures prove to be the answer to the basic problem which is getting the pike to take it in the first place. All lures work at one time or another, but generally on the waters I fish they are an inefficient method of catching pike. Because on waters such as Blithfield they are the only option we just have to get on with it.

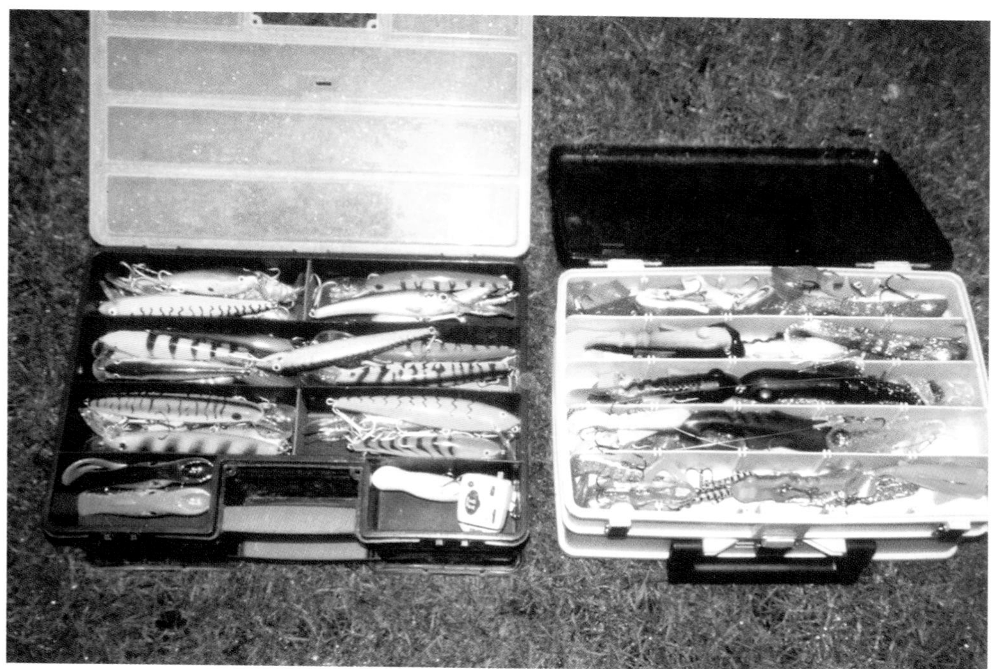

My lures boxes - left: home made double box, two flat boxes pop riveted together right: plano box - more than enough lures!

I'm not one for having an immense selection of lures though I still have about 50 in my lure box. This I've made by pop riveting two B&Q tool boxes together back to back. The mega serious lure anglers may carry a hundred lures, but looking at how one or two of these have performed on waters such as Blithfield it does not appear to have done them any good. Lure fishing on a trout water is probably different from on Windermere or in the Baltic. I'm sure lure selection can at times be important on big pressured waters. On Blithfield however lures are so ineffective that we are probably catching only a handful of the pike and certainly not twice. So on this water any decent lure is in with a chance. The same applied on Ladybower and to some extent on waters such as Rutland Water

My main line of attack as far as lures are concerned consists of soft lures, spoons and crankbaits. The old favourites the Bulldawg and Springdawgs may have had a lot of use, but they still catch pike. I'd always have some of these in my collection. I'm not too fussed about the colours; I generally like the less garish colours. The Cisco colour is a favourite and I've also had a fair number of takes on the walleye pattern of Shallow Dawg.

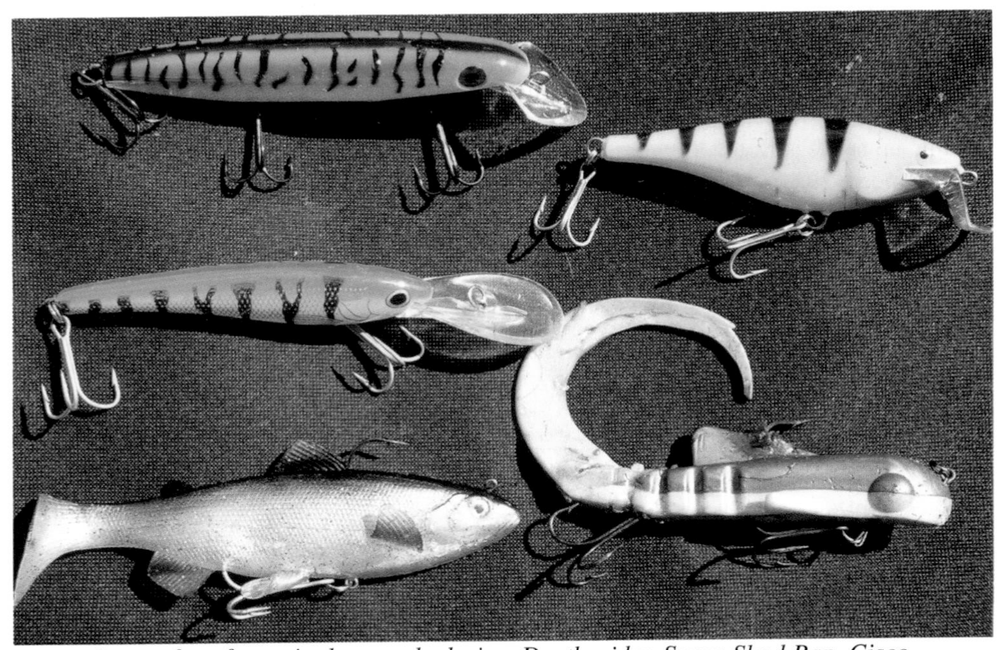

Some of my favourite lures - clockwise: Depthraider, Super Shad Rap, Cisco, Bulldawg, Fox Replicant and Storm Deep Thunder

(This one I actually caught at Vastervick in Sweden!).There are other similar designs about now including Fox's Deviant and Masterline's reservoir Dawg. Most of the pike I have caught on Dawgs have come from trout waters. Though I think they are wonderful lures there is no telling whether or not I would have caught the same pike on another lure. The best day I ever had with lures was with Neville Fickling on Ladybower. At the time the result we had had was so good we didn't dare claim the catch from the code name water "Masons". Instead we had to invent another water and named it in honour of Des Taylor who had tried to guess where Masons was! We called it "Taylors"! The result at the end of the day was six twenties to Neville and four to me. Most came on Springdawgs with the odd fish on spoons. The significant fact was that none of the lures were large and though we dropped the odd fish off we would have probably lost a lot more if we had used big baits. We just happened to pick a good selection of lures for pike which had probably never seen a lure before and were up for it. You have to remember that Ladybower pike dine well from March to November while trout stocks are high. As the months pass the trout stocks gradually decline and by the months of January and February the pike are a bit peckish. We just happened to find a pile of pike on the right day with some effective lures.

On another lake called Stoneacres the pike in this water responded to Replicants and I managed a brace of twenties from there in one day followed by another from one of Jason Davis's waters. The Stoneacre pike were once trout fed, but now the trout were long gone. In the real world they should have taken live or deadbaits, but as so often happens in pike fishing they decided to take something daft like a lure!

would be coupled with a multiplier with the line as tight as possible. The reel would be in free spool with the casting tension set to just counter the drag of the water. The rod tips would be at least a foot under the surface so the wind didn't pull line off. The 30mm butt ring was pushed right up to the alarm so the line couldn't skip over the wheel when I had a take. I had a number of twenties to over 25lb in a very short space of time. Other pike anglers kept complaining that I was not using drop offs, but I never let them know why. They were getting bobbins dropping off, but then they had dropped runs. What happened with my set up was that if a pike pulled line from any angle, because of the heavy flattened lead it had to pull line from the reel. The resistance from the reel was as near as consistent as could be managed in these circumstances. It paid off because dropped runs were much reduced and of course I had soon caught a nice pile of fish with very little competition from other anglers.When the pike moved after Christmas to the start of the arms they could then be reached by casting. This made fishing more straight forward and of course as the end of the season approached the pike moved shallower and shallower.

On the Staffs Reservoir we had the benefit of boats and you could go anywhere. These pike became finicky as well and it was then that I used the hair rig extensively. Towards the backend the pike would move into the shallows where boats were not allowed. This would then see me bank fishing. I would use my chest waders to wade out beyond the marginal reeds and find a clear area. There I would lower a bait. The float was set up at the exact depth with a couple of swan shot to hold the deadbait in position. The bait was rigged up with a single size 1 Super Specialist to a wire trace with a piece of Dacron with a loop tied and silicon tubed to the hook shank. The loop was then pushed through the nose of the bait with a boily needle and when the loop was pulled through I'd attach a small snaplink and this would be clipped back onto the braid. When you had a run you'd simply give it a bit longer and you'd hook them in the scissors. My biggest doing this was 26-10.

On some reservoirs you really need to get away from angling pressure. Stanford Reservoir in Northamptonshire was a good example. The shallow areas on this reservoir were out of bounds to the public, but luckily for me a friend of mine worked for Severn Trent and they could fish from a small area there. We had a good day there once with about 12 doubles including three twenty pounders.

The largest of all natural waters in England are in the Lake District. The situation has changed a lot there since I started fishing. In those days Windermere was still netted and there appeared to be no pike worth mentioning anywhere else. Then Esthwaite became well known as a trout water which produced some big fish, but sadly a lot of fish died due to poor handling. I fished there 3 or 4 times and caught a few small ones and the odd double. I more or less discounted the Lake District after that, until Winderemere started producing. I've not visited many times, but I have had a couple of twenty pounders there. It is an ideal place to take the big boat (that is until the speed restrictions are imposed). The variety of depths from which pike can be taken on this water makes it interesting fishing. You are however restricted in your methods to dead-baiting and lure fishing. This is a shame, but the EA has legislated against the use of livebaits and natural deadbaits.

Windermere is a lake full of features. During the course of a day's static fishing, even half a dozen moves will have only stratched the surface of the available swims. On Windermere you can catch out of 40 feet of water, off of points jutting out from the bank, from submerged plateaux and on the edge of drop offs. There is so much structure there and of course the water is full of roach and other food fish. You simply have to try as many swims as possible. Windermere pike also have a reputation of being active after dark and plenty of twenty pounders have been caught in winter after dark. It pays to have navigation lights on your boat because the last time I fished into the dark I got pulled by the water police. Luckily they let me off with a warning so now I'll have to fit some lights.

Our big rivers present special problems, mainly having to cope with the fast flow typical of waters such as the Wye and the Severn. If you cast a bait out on one of these rivers the current does everything possible to push your bait into the edge often with a suitable adornment of weed and assorted debris. My introduction to the Wye was via Ron Baker the well known match angler who I have mentioned earlier. In the late seventies the Wye around Hereford was full of 12oz chub and it was not unusual for the match anglers to have these taken on the way in. Despite these obvious signs I didn't get down there until 1981-82 which was still well before most other people became interested in the Wye's big pike.

It took me a while to realise exactly what water conditions were conducive to good fishing on the Wye. Ron Baker told me that 3ft 10ins of extra water at Hereford was the key and of course he was absolutely right. Once I started to fish in these conditions my catch rate improved. I didn't catch anything huge, but at least I was encountering a few fish to mid doubles.

A friend of mine had a salmon beat at King's Caple and he had seen a monster pike which even then was enough to get me seriously interested. He had seen this fish lying up against a salmon croy. These were artificial structures built out into the river to deflect the current and in so doing provide spots for salmon to lay up as they made their way upstream. They also provided ideal fishing stations for the salmon anglers and of course the odd pike angler such as me. I went down and gave it a go and the first fish I had was 23lb followed by a 17 pounder. My friend insisted that neither of these fish was the big one. King's Caple consisted of about 600 yards of water, firstly shallow with a six foot deeper area. There were plenty of overhanging bushes and of course the salmon croys. Long Croy was where the big pike was said to live, but alas our paths were not to cross. The swim was below a point and here there was a deep spot of around 12 feet deep. When the river was higher, other croys were worth fishing because the croys used to push the main flow out into the river.

30-09 Staffordshire Reservoir

30-12 Staffordshire Reservoir

My second thirty pounder also happened to be my one and only repeat capture of a very big fish. Having caught the 32-02 it was simply a case of carrying on with the fishing on a water that was getting better all the time. Despite this it was still hard going catching twenty pounders. It wasn't until March 13th, the day before the end of the season that I caught another big fish. I was out in the boat trolling on the oars using two deadbaits. One was a grayling caught recently from the River Teme, the other was a roach. The unlucky grayling ended up as bait because everywhere had been frozen up and grayling fishing was about all there was worth fishing for. It was a really foggy day and I was doing my best to find my way. Unfortunately my direction finding was not all that it should have been. The result was a grinding noise as the boat scrunched onto a gravel bar by the bank. The rod with the roach was nearest the bank so I wound it in. I then went to wind in the other rod, but the float was already trundling away. Something had taken the bait in only three or four feet of water. When I struck the pike boiled on the surface before charging off. As is so often the case these cold water pike are very slow movers which gave me time to put my foot over the side of the boat and push myself out into deeper water. There it was a straightforward job to net the fish. Even while I was playing the fish I recognised which one it was. By this time it had a very humpty backed look to it and it was without doubt the 32-02. For some daft reason we ended up nick-naming that fish Gertie the thirty.

The fog lifted at that moment, just as I was weighing her. Because I was on my own I had to get someone from the bank to photograph her. Unfortunately she had probably partially spawned since I last caught her and weighed 30-12. It was actually quite normal for the pike in this water to spawn in late February. The following October she was caught at 23-08, gradually increasing to 26-08 and then she dissappeared.

In the years that followed I continued to catch some more twenty pounders from the reservoir up to 26-10. I was not lucky enough to encounter any of the fish that later grew on to 35-12. There were some amazing weight fluctuations with these fish. I remember one 22 pounder caught in October turning up in February at 31lb plus. It is also interesting that this was one of the few waters to receive trout water pike that actually survived and did well.

30-12 Tong Mere

Tong Mere is one of the meres on the edge of Shropshire and Staffordshire. It was built by Capability Brown and is on Lord Bradford's estate, Weston under Lizzard. It is a 38 acre estate lake and one which I had been visiting since I was twelve. It was typical, of this type of water, shallow at the inlet end and deeper at the dam end. It was beautifully landscaped with Rhododendrons fringing the lake and acres of woodland. Being only 14 miles from my house it was worth a look as a pike water having done fish to 26-08 about ten years earlier. Before I describe the capture of the big pike we had an interesting method of catching livebaits. Lots of roach used to shelter under the punts and the way to catch them was to rock the punt. This scared the fish and as they came out of the boathouse you simply scooped them out with the landing net! Oh that catching livebaits was always as easy!

30-09 and 22-06 brace, Tong Mere

This water was another that received trout water pike. Blithfield in those days operated a pike removal program. So once again I became involved in a one man pike rescue operation. Fish up to 33-02 were moved and a year later I caught a fish at 30-09 which had been stocked at 31-06. Another of only a few examples of trout water pike doing OK in a non trout water.

The day I caught the fish I was fishing with Robbie Harrison and we were set up on the bank on the point at the deep end. We were paternostering live roach in about 10 feet of water. We had been there for the first unproductive couple of hours. Then I had the first run which was 22-04. I got the livebait back and recast into the same spot catching the 30-09 after about 10 minutes. Robbie had a couple of doubles so lady luck was smiling on me that day. Obviously after a day like that I had to go back, but it was not to be. I was there and netted the other thirty for three different people when it weighed around 32-08. Incidentally the 32-08 was Des Taylor's personal best pike. I had fished the Mere on Sunday catching a 22-12. A chap in the next swim was just about to pack up before 1pm and I was actually praying that he'd go because I thought the big girl might come out. Sure enough he caught her leaving me only with the job of netting and weighing her. He only had one rod out by then!

I returned on Wednesday and had a 28-02 in the morning which was a native fish. Then I hooked the thirty midday and played her right to the net where the hooks pulled out! That evening Des Taylor rang me up to see how I had got on. He had planned to go roach fishing, but the river was up. He asked if he0 could go to Tong Mere with me the next day. Always happy to accommodate the big hairy one I agreed. He arrived the next morning with no traces and no bait (typical roach angler, typical Des). I put him in the swim where I had lost the pike. Within one hour he had had a 21 and a 32-06. I nearly keeled over when I netted the big one for the third time, but time is a great healer and now I can look back with some amusement. Des in celebration took my wife and I out for a slap up meal.

Interestingly these Blithfield pike were soon weaned onto deadbaits, something they were always slow to respond to in their natural habitat. Des caught his fish on a deadbait from a swim which had regularly been prebaited. Blithfield pike behaved in a similar manner in other waters and it is clear that having vast numbers of trout swimming around them while in their native water caused them to have no interest in deadbaits. I've heard all sorts of stories about ex Blithfield pike. Some simply faded away when stocked into waters incapable of supporting them. Others grew bigger and behaved partly like a Blithfield pike, i.e. they chased moving baits, but unlike the pike in its natural home also liked deadbaits.

In later years those big pike succumbed to poor angling techniques and with Blithfield no longer removing big pike there was no longer a supply of big pike to compensate. The Mere still produces pike to 24lb and who knows what might still be lurking in there.

32-08 Lough Derravaragh

Gary Banks returning a 27-08

A big pike near the end of the fight

we arrived at the bay we had a rummage through the freezer box, the contents of which were looking at bit sparse and worse for wear. The boy picked up this huge herring, quite sensibly thought better of it so I stuck it on instead. At the time I was still fishing with telescopic rods, but such was the weight of the herring that I had to telescope the top two sections so I could hopefully lob the bait a few yards away from the boat.

We had several doubles and I had another low twenty. Needless to say the big herring hadn't moved. Then totally unexpectedly at 11am the clicker on the multiplier reel indicated that I either had a tope run or more likely a big fast moving pike. Striking more in hope, somehow I connected with her. She tail walked straight away throwing the herring out and no doubt providing a meal for the next week for another lucky pike. Then after a very strong fight the boy made no mistake with the net. Irish thirty pounders despite what you might hear are not that common. Being an optimist I had always hoped to come across one, but in the back of my mind I knew it was a long shot. Yet there on the mat in the bottom of the boat was a spawned out 32 pounder. It was about 47 inches long the length of a number of pike over 35lb. With that I reeled in and went to sleep in the bottom of the boat until it was time to go home.

40-12 Bluebell

The Bluebell gravel pit complex at Tansor between Peterborough and Northampton is today better known for its very large carp. There was a time though when it held one of the biggest pike in the country. This particular fish first appeared in the early 90s and weighed 34lb. Its captor should have been quite well known, but despite appearing in the angling press seems to have been forgotten. As is so often the case the person who makes the most noise gets the credit for a first capture. Derek MacDonald of Corby was incorrectly credited with the first known capture of the fish at 31lb. It was said to have been caught on a lure. gradually the fish got bigger and bigger until it eventually reached 41-12 This was caught by Colin Bailey in February of 1995 My first visit to the complex was when some big pike had been stocked into Swan Lake from Grafham. Eddie Turner (ET), Dave Phillips and I decided to give it a go. I caught lots of fish, but nothing bigger than 17lb. ET had a 21 pounder and then returned a few days later and landed a 30. While we were there we discussed whether or not to have a go for the forty in the pit next-door. ET later had a go, but I never bothered. I was too busy fishing at Bough Beech.

By this time Brian Ingram had caught the big Bluebell pike at 37lb so I thought no more about it. As luck would have it we had a freeze up and then Des Taylor was looking to do a pike fishing feature for Sky's Tight Lines. The only place we could think of which wouldn't be frozen was the River Nene where it runs through the Bluebell complex. With the filming out of the way I was trying to think of what to do with the one day I had to spare before I went to Lough Mask with one of Neville's groups of anglers. It had started to get mild so I thought I'd have a go for the forty pounder. The impulse was as sudden as that. A few days later I made my first fishing visit to Kingfisher Lake. At the time there was only two double figure pike in the water and it was thought that the

40-12 Bluebell Lake

smaller fish of around 13lb had gone anyway. When I arrived the lake was clear of ice, the wind was a nice south westerly and there was only one other angler on the lake. He was the somewhat unfortunate Carl Allen who had fished the lake regularly in the hope of catching the big one, but was never quite lucky enough. I set up with three rods, two deadbaits and a free roving livebait. The day started slowly as was to be expected with three very small pike.

I was speaking to Carl Allen and he was telling me that the big one didn't tend to come out until the afternoon. I jokingly said "I'll catch it at 3pm this afternoon. (I wish I had kept my big mouth shut, poor Carl!). I started in the corner with the wind off my back drifting a livebait, then I started to move to the left around the lake. With the wind going from right to left I opted to use the Microcat radio controlled boat to drop the free roving half pound roach about 70 yards out in the middle of the lake. In this way I could cover a lot of water before I needed to repeat the process. On the second attempt the float dissappeared and when I wound down I thought I'd hooked a small pike stuck in the weed. It was too heavy to be just a pike. As I gained line it moved off to the right. Jacks in weed do not do this. It then came up on the surface and I could see clearly that this was the one. I hoped with all my heart that the hooks did not fall out! Any normal pike would have been easy to land single handed, but this one was so deep that I was in danger of it beaching if I brought it too close to the bank. Instead I almost had to drag it into the landing net holding the rod high over my shoulder.

Now this fishing for known fish may remove the element of the unknown when you are fishing. Take it from me though, when you hook the target fish first trip your emotions range from dread that you going to lose it to amazement that you've caught it so quickly, without having to indure the dozens of blanks expected. Once in the net I unhooked her there and then carried her to near my van and put her in a tube. The weighing should have been straight forward, but whenever any person of normal stature catches a fish near 40lbs holding the scales steady presents problems. To get an accurate weight I supported the Reuben Heaton 60lb scales with a bank stick and allowed the vans back door to support one end of the bank stick. In this way everything was steady. A weight of 40-12 was recorded. I then slipped her back into the tube and phoned Angling Times and Anglers Mail. Mick Rouse and Dave Phillips respectively arrived within 15 minutes. After that I never fished Kingfisher again. Interestingly a photograph of my big pike with someone else's head attached ended up on a website advertising Alaskan pike fishing. Such is the dodgy behaviour you can now expect in certain parts of the world. That was the last time that particular pike was caught. She died over a year later and is now in a glass case at the fishery.

Tony Bridgefoot the owner came round to congratulate me and a while later it dawned on me that it was not a day ticket water but infact a syndicate. So in reality I shouldn't have been there in the first place. Whoops! Waters with just the odd big pike in them are fairly uncommon and catching one fish from such a water can be a time consuming and frustrating experience. To grow to 40lbs a pike needs a decent food supply and in Kingfisher it probably consisted of other pike, good sized tench, roach and even chub.

When the Bluebell pike died Tony Bridgefoot had the fish set-up so she will be more than just a memory

The key requirement is suitable prey that a big pike does not have to chase itself silly to catch. If that pike has the water too itself and does not have to compete with other big pike it is going to grow to a fair old size. Such situations have up to now been happy accidents. Perhaps from now on some enterprising fishery owner will realise that the odd big pike even in a heavily small carp fishery could prove a big attraction in the winter.

30-08 River Adur

The River Adur in West Sussex is not perhaps the best known pike fishery in the country, but over a period of time I had become aware of its potential. An invitation from "Polish" Joe Raczkowski saw me heading south. Another 195 mile journey with a 6am meeting saw me leave home at 3am. The only advantage of travelling at this time is that there is no-one else on the road at this time. When I arrived I got out of the van and the cold took my breath away. With the chill factor it felt about minus 10. Not typical weather for March 13th. To add to my woes one look at the river with its narrowness and the pebbles on the bottom showing was enough to half convince me to go home.

Then Polish Joe arrived full of enthusiasm and we set off upstream leap frogging. My first cast with a paternostered livebait ended up in about 4 foot of water. There was not enough water to submerge my sunken float. The 12 foot rods were almost touching the other bank. Still I was there now and I thought I'd give it a try, find out it was waste of time and go home. After about 3 hours of leap frogging Joe had the first run, a

The bridge swim on the River Adur which produced my thirty

30-08 River Adur

beautiful pristine 21 pounder. By the end of the afternoon we had seen nothing else so I persuaded Joe to go back to the car. I was going to bivvy up on the bank so Joe suggested just below the bridge where I could also fish through the night. Out went two deadbaits and a livebait. Before I had set my bivvy up the livebait drop off had come off. I thought a duck had run into the line, when I picked the rod up and wound down it was clear that this was no duck. The water erupted in front of me and next thing I realised was that my net wasn't set up. I shouted Joe and he quickly appeared and set the net up. Before he netted it he was telling me in no uncertain manner that it was a thirty pounder. Safely in the net it was clear that he was right. She weighed 30-08, my first pike ever from the water, on a first visit! I fished through the night had a twelve pounder at midnight, fished all next day with Joe for no result and never returned.

The Adur is an interesting river because it is tidal, has a run of seatrout, mullet investigate its lower reaches and it has a big roach stock. I do not think that there are huge numbers of pike present, which is probably why it is such slow going. Then again the quality of the pike easily compensates for the lack of action.

31-08 Hampshire Avon

If the River Adur is not well known for big pike the Hampshire Avon certainly is. I had never fished the river before though as a kid brought up on Mr. Crabtree I had certainly read about fishing such a river. For someone from the West Midlands Bernard Venables description of fast flowing rivers with deep pools and overhanging trees bore little resemblance to waters near where I lived. I had often thought about pike fishing the Avon and certainly there were enough big pike reported from there to whet my appetite.

One day while at work a chance conversation with Richard Howard led to him suggesting I have a go on the Parlour Pool which opened that week. This just happened to be on my regular fishing days (Tuesday and Wednesday). He told me where to get the day ticket. After another really early start I was soon realising that this trip might be a mistake. The wind was howling, there were trees down and I had already convinced myself the river would be in flood. Despite this I was soon walking out of the shop clutching my day ticket and driving off to find this most famous of Hampshire Avon swims.

On arriving I walked down to what I'd been told was the best swim, where the Parlour joined the main river. There was someone already there. So I walked back to the top of the Parlour and walked down the other side of a six foot high fence. The rain was bad and though the river was slightly coloured a feeder stream was even more coloured. Because of this my original choice of swim which was occupied did not inspire me much anyway. So I fished upstream of all the dirty water in the Parlour itself. As luck would have it a lot of pike had piled into the area as I was soon to find out. There is a strict no livebaiting rule on the water and because it is strictly baliffed I wasn't going to chance it. Neville Fickling had recently supplied me with some lamprey baits which had done well on a number of waters. So I put one lamprey head section out, a dead roach

31-08 Hampshire Avon

The Parlour swim on the Hampshire Avon

The Hampshire Avon was kind to me, this 26-08 on lamprey came with a 31-08

and a smelt, all float legered. The beauty of lamprey of course is the constant steam of blood that leaks out of the bait. If a pike is feeding by smell the water soluble blood must surely give out a trail a pike can home onto. It certainly ought to be more effective than the oils you get in say sardines which probably float away.

I was eating my breakfast at 9am when the indicator pulled off and the float dissappeared. I was soon looking at a 26-08 pike. That had taken the lamprey. Getting the lamprey back I put the pike in the tube and quickly squashed the lamprey before casting it back out. I went to the fence and called the other angler asking him to come and photograph the fish. Instead of walking about 200 yards along the fence he popped through a hole I hadn't realised existed. I had walked all that way when there was a shortcut. Having returned the fish I sat down to finish my breakfast. Then the indicator dropped off again and off the float trundled. On winding down all hell let loose as a very angry pike charged off. I landed it myself and soon realised that this one was bigger than the first. A lot bigger at 31-08. I was almost having to pinch myself at this stage. I recast the same bait again, had another run and pulled out of it. Then an hour later I had my final run and that went 19-14. A very economical use of baits!

Feeling now that my good fortune was running particularly strongly I went the next day to the Dorset Stour at Warminster and this time holed out with just a few small ones. Sometimes when you try to ride your luck it does not always work out! Despite this the result I had on the Avon was another first session wonder and readers might be starting to think that I'm so lucky that they could never emulate my success. However when you think about it any good day is a combination of factors. What is important is to be able to recognise those factors. Firstly Richard Howard had tipped me off about the Parlour swim opening that week. Being first on a water after a break is always useful. On that day I fished the clear water rather than the hot swim. The bait was something that was probably new on this water which ought to be helpful on pressured waters. Also I didn't mention that there was one tree on the far bank with new leaves on it. This tree was protected from the cold north east winds by a house on the island and all fish prefer to live in as stable an environment as they can find. This was why instead of one big pike you end up with several in the one area. Each pike is looking for somewhere comfortable with access to food and each pike independently recognises a favoured spot.

Having no other good clues as to where to fish next I had reasoned that my swim was not going to produce again the 2nd day so I went elsewhere. There is always a chance that making a move is going to be a terrible mistake. Luckily I seem to get it right more often than wrong, but I still do make mistakes.

33-14 Swangey

It was sometime around 1998 that I saw the Swangey fish in the Anglers Mail. Having had some success with one known fish, the Bluebell pike I thought that maybe I could do something with this one. Jason Davies had already caught her at 30lb plus and while a few other pike anglers were after her at least I could roll up midweek. Needless to say

once again it was an early start. The two of us met Alan, obtained some trout livebaits and headed off to Fairholmes to bank fish. Neville had obviously been there before, but for me it was a bit of a strange situation. We were fishing slap on the end of a great big car park complete with rangers office, burger bar and visitors centre. At weekends all through the year the place was alive with people. Fortunately our condition of fishing saw us there midweek only. Parking the vans as near as possible we staggered down the steep banks and put rod rests in. Now Neville had an idea where he wanted his rods, so I just put one each on the outside of his two. We were going to livebait with two rods each and then lure fish between the rods.

It was blowing a bit of a gale, sufficient to blow the tea out of my cup and things got off to a slow start. The first fish we had were small, but I think there was a twelve pounder amongst them. Then totally accidentally (though Neville often wonders about this) I managed to get one of my lines tangled up with his. The damage I did to his gear was such that I was recast ten minutes before he was fishing again. Then my Fox Micron drop off sounded and I ran helter skelter down the slope to my rod. Line was running out and because the trout baits were only 2 to 3oz I wound down straight away. This one was obviously not another small pike. It didn't do very much on the way to the net, but the most striking thing from where I was standing ten foot above Neville and the net was its colour. It was an amazing light colour and while I'm sure my memory is playing tricks with me I'd swear it looked like a great big banana as it came in. Neville netted her and he too remarked on its unusual colour. He also remarked on its weight. It took two of us to stagger up the bank with it in the net. It had to be a

A quiet and cold afternoon on Ladybower

thirty pounder and it was so incredibly fat. Here was a pike that had dined almost to excess on rainbow trout for perhaps 7 or 8 years.

We weighed her at 33-14, but forgot to measure her. Within a few minutes she was photographed and returned. Like all the Ladybower thirties we had between us (8) we never saw her again. Yet again the first day lucky charm had worked. Don't ask me how it works though. The rest of the day passed with no more big fish, but Neville who had been wasting his time with Bulldawgs and Springdawgs suddenly started to get takes and ended up with about half a dozen doubles to 17lb. I was then left with the terrible journey through Glossop, the outskirts of Manchester and the dreaded M6. I was not unhappy despite this!

31-08 Ladybower

My second thirty pounder from Ladybower came because of a combination of events. Most importantly Neville was away in Ireland that week. Up until this time we had not explored the reservoir that much. While Neville had previously caught the 37-08 from the end of the Snake arm we were still giving the Fairholmes area the greatest part of our attention. So obviously on this two day trip that was where I started. Initially I had a couple of hours off the car park, but didn't have a run. So I moved to where a small stream comes in and while casting a Springdawg caught a 20-02 pike. I photographed the fish myself, well pleased with my first lure caught twenty pounder. I then moved back to the car park and tried the lure there, but with no result so then it was time to

Ladybower in extreme conditions, but you'd still catch if you could get there

31-08 and 25-02 brace Ladybower

move lock stock and barrel to where I had just caught the twenty. Initially I cast around with a Springdawg and I had two follows in two casts. I immediately cast in two paternostered livebaits and I was away straight away. That went 31-08 so I put it in a tube so I could fetch a ranger to photograph the fish. I never got that far because the other was away and that was 25-02. Now with no rods left in the water I ran off to get a ranger who did me proud with the photographs. Luckily he had been a photographer in the RAF.

To add to my excitement the ranger said that he had seen bigger fish than those in the edges in the summer. I carried on fishing and had a couple of small fish and had to go see Alan to get some more livebaits. I continued the next day and by fishing a variety spots managed a 19-04 on a Springdawg. However as is so often the case on Ladybower, once you've had a good catch from a swim it takes a good week to recover. At the time we were fishing during that 1st year water levels were almost always high. While at the Snake end of the reservoir coloured water was a regular feature, where we fished at Fairholmes the water was nearly always crystal clear. This is because the water flowed down from the dam above where the Derwent reservoir acted as a giant settling pond.

Between the three of us fishing we had not caught a huge number of pike, but we already had three thirties in the bag. All were different fish and we constantly speculated on how big the pike could get. We felt that there was no reason why this water could not give Llandegfedd a run for its money. It was not to be the case.

30-12 Ladybower

The following season on Ladybower saw us take to the boat more often. We had 8 twenties the previous winter and though three were thirties we started to think that we were not getting the best out of the water. It was early December and we had tried Fairholmes the first day. I had had one follow on a Mr Muskie spoon which I was sure was a good fish, but I somehow forgot to tell Neville about it! The next day we were afloat at the Snake River end trolling lures. We were chugging along some overhanging trees when Neville's Bulldawg was hit hard. Unfortunately it came off just as I was letting a bit more line out on my Super Shad. Then suddenly something hit my lure while I struggled to close the bale arm. That one went 27-06. Later in the day Neville decided to go home in order to avoid the traffic in Sheffield. Rush hour in that city can add an hour to the journey home. I had to decide whether or not to stay with the boat fishing, but in the end I opted to have the last few hours as Fairholmes. I didn't have an instant run, but the way the livebaits were working suggested that something evil was lurking down there. Eventually after 45 minutes whatever it was decided that enough was enough and snaffled my livebait. With relatively little drama I netted a 30lb 12oz pike. At the time this fish with the 27-06 was my biggest brace.

30-12 Ladybower

Low water levels were interesting on Ladybower

31-10 Ladybower

My fourth thirty pounder from Ladybower came about when Neville was away again. The week previously we had finally had the big catch we had dreamed of. We had been boat fishing up the Snake Arm and had shared a catch of 10 twenties all on lures. Unfortunately it had rained a lot while we were there and rained a lot more afterwards. Interestingly that day Neville had had a follow off of a pike which turned and all he got was a glimpse of its tail. He thought it was bigger than anything we had caught that day. I really expected to have a repeat performance of the previous week, but when I arrived the boat was locked up and there was no sign of Alan. Luckily I keep a few tools in the car and soon had the lock off and was on my way up the Snake Arm. The rain was absolutely lashing down and when I arrived at the good area the water was more coloured than I had ever seen before. Visibility was zero and my hopes of a good day vaporised. I tried lure fishing, but it looked a total no hoper. Then I trolled livebaits on the electric motor and had one offer from a jack which came off.

I took the electric motor off the back and decided to go to Fairholmes bank fishing. I then wound in one rod and picked the other one up. The float had gone, but because I was drifting I thought I was snagged and the float had pulled under. It wasn't the case though because as I wound in and pulled something pulled back. Luckily I had left the landing net up as something rather large loomed out of the murky water. I was close to the bank so with the pike in the net I was able to sort everything out including my first self taken photographs of a 30 pounder. She weighed 31-10 and had some very pretty markings on her head, totally unlike the other pike we had caught.

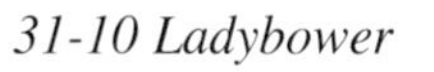

31-10 Ladybower

This incident just goes to show what a disadvantage we operate under when fishing trout waters without access to livebaits. I'm sure I could have lure fished until I dropped for no result. Even with a livebait it was going to be hard work, but on that day one little bait fish made the difference between success and failure.

32-06 Blithfield

As I write Blithfield is still the water which has produced more 35lb plus pike than any other in Great Britain and Ireland. I do not think there was any way to predict that this 800 acre trout reservoir was going to be this good. Certainly how it all came about was more by accident than anything else. For as long as I can remember Blithfield has been run by Blithfield Anglers. It has been heavily stocked with trout for many years and has a good head of coarse fish including roach around 12 to 16oz, big dace and perch. Pike first appeared at Blithfield in the mid seventies and for a few years no-one paid much attention to them. Indeed if anyone asked about pike, blank looks were likely to be your answer. As the decade turned, pike started to become more evident. Blithfield Anglers decided to have a members pike fishing weekend. The result of this was a lot of pike caught to low twenties, almost all of which were killed. My first visit probably around that time in I think November of 1983 was a complete waste of time. Not surprisingly considering I was fishing with two deadbaits! Everything that was caught came on lures and not the sophisticated lures we see today. A 28g Toby and a Big S was all you needed.

The Lure Blankers club at Blithfield

32-06 Blithfield

The next weekend it opened half the serious pike anglers in the country were there or so it seemed. Now I was fishing as a guest of a trout fishing friend of mine called Jack Davies while half this new influx of anglers had appeared from no-where. There seemed to be no control over what was going on and it later transpired that I spot on there with people who should know better knocking an 8lb brownie on the head and taking it home. I ended up having a strong disagreement with Norman Spiers (the president of the club) and Mike Reay (the fishery manager). I threw my tackle in the truck and went home. All in all not the most auspicious start to my period of fishing Blithfield. It was going to get a lot worse than this before it got better.

When I got home I wondered whether I'd gone too far, but in the end I decided that I had done the right thing. I may not be whiter than white a lot of the time, but in this instance I felt that allowing a free for all with uninvited people fishing and livebaits being smuggled onto the water would sooner or later see the pike fishing lost for good.

Norman Spiers and I had known each other since I was 16 so though we had had cross words I wasn't without hope that we would eventually see eye to eye. In the meantime I continued to trout fish it as a guest of my friend. Without wishing to tell everyone I told them so, someone was caught livebaiting and it became clear that uninvited anglers were turning up some of which didn't even pay. To add to this the parasite *Ergasalis* turned up and the pike anglers were immediately blamed. Up until this time a lot of pike up to 31lb had been caught most of which were transferred to loads of different waters.

Everyone gathered for the off at Blithfield

For some time, I think a couple of years there was no pike fishing, then Blithfield Anglers decided to allow members only to fish for the pike. Only a handful of guests were allowed, it was much more strictly controlled and it was lure only. All the pike my friends and I caught could be moved while the rest were killed. One angler had nine twenty pounders in one day. This included 3 thirties another 5 over 25lbs and one tiddler of 22lbs which were all killed and taken home. My group of friends had a 33-03, 31-06, 27-12, 27-08 and smaller twenties which were transferred. Unfortunately one misguided individual put a 12 pounder back and was seen doing so and the pike fishing ceased again.

I then tried writing to Norman Spiers via Mike Reay to try and set up some proper pike fishing. According to Norman he never received those letters. I then joined Blithfield Anglers as a half season member which entitled me to two days fishing in November and the right to take a guest. During the second year as a member Norman asked me to a meeting at the fishing lodge. The subject would be pike fishing at Blithfield. We agreed on a syndicate of around 25 members plus three or four of the full trout members who were really there only for the pike fishing. £300 may at the time have seemed a lot of money for 8 days fishing, but later events were to prove that it was good value for money.

The invitations went out to a number of keen pike anglers, most of which accepted. The letter that went out was the same as the one which went out before and here was the crux of the matter. That letter said that all pike under 25lb had to be removed. That did not concern me unduly because I had had the same letter the year before and had been able to return pike under 25lb with the knowledge of Mike Reay without any problems. That year most of the pike anglers present did the same and very few pike were killed. In effect we had reached the turning point. We had gone from a situation where pike were being killed on a regular basis to one where it was an unusual event.

Then the news broke and it seemed as if the whole pike fishing world were up in arms. Press releases arrived at Angling Times, yet no-one talked to me or Blithfield Anglers. While all this was going on a home had been found for any pike which were to be removed and we were not far from convincing Blithfield Anglers that if they wanted to charge £300 for 8 days fishing the pike would have to be returned. The whole sorry mess ended up getting totally out of hand and though it was resolved in the end, it didn't help the cause of pike conservation at all. While the intentions of those involved may well have been honourable, there is a lot to be said for waiting and giving a little breathing space before you wade in all guns blazing.

The first years fishing was bank only and as was to be expected some of the favourite spots such as Watery Lane had pike anglers queuing for the 7am off. Amazingly there were no silly tantrums or disagreement amongst the members. Those that were willing to muck in at Watery Lane were generally disappointed, but big fish were caught during most of the two day sessions. Enough to get a lot people coming back for more. I tried wandering around here and there trying to emulate the free spirited anglers who seemed to catch good fish from unlikely areas and though I caught the odd double, I could not catch even a twenty pounder, let along a thirty. As far as I can remember there were no 35lb plus pike caught that winter. Despite the lack of monster pike, nearly everyone came back for more. Additional members joined as the syndicate was expanded.

The second year was a mixture of bank and boat fishing. The rush for Watery Lane was on again and Mick Brown was the lucky angler with a 35 pounder. The fact that anything was caught was a miracle because we had experienced non stop rain for many days. The water was like tea, the reservoir was at its highest recorded level and many people struggled to get there. Paul Mardle must have thought he was driving a submarine when in his efforts to get to Blithfield he flooded his Cavalier. James Gardner nearly came a cropper too, but for several of us being prepared to strip our socks, shoes and trousers off to push his old estate out of a patch of deep water. Water conditions did not improve much that season, but the pike just got bigger. Jason Davies 37 pounder was another fish caught in adverse water condition and at one stage it was looking as if nothing would prevent at least one big pike turning up in a session. Of course the odd big pike sounds wonderful on paper and the person who caught it no doubt celebrated. That however does not take into account the other 50 odd people that didn't catch a 37 pounder. When conditions were dire at Blithfield most people struggled.

The third season started with conditions being good, but set to deteriorate. It started to rain once the fishing had started and within a day the water would start to colour up. Eric Edwards rewrote the record books with the biggest brace ever on rod and line in the UK, a 37 and a 41-08. To some extent that was probably the peak, but there were still plenty of big pike to be caught the following season. It almost got to the stage where if you caught a thirty it would go 35lb.

Everyone had expected the fourth season to produce a pike to nudge the UK record. It didn't happen though. For all that the 35lb plus pike kept coming, but studies carried out by Jason Davies threw up some interesting facts. He had been collecting photographs of 30lb pike from the reservoir since it had first opened. Using the now well known technique of using the characteristic markings of pike to match up recaptures, he found that only one 35lb plus pike had been a recapture and that was at a lower weight. No 35lb plus fish had been caught twice. It is possible to speculate as to why this was and a number of explanations come to light. Firstly one could suggest that none of the big pike survived after having been caught. Now while it is true that not all dead pike float to the surface, some do. It is hard to imagine that every big Blithfield pike died and none were washed into the shore. A better explanation to my mind was that the method used to catch these pike was hopelessly inefficient. Work carried out in Holland years ago showed that pike rapidly wised up to lures. It would not be unreasonable to assume that a big Blithfield pike once caught on a lure would be less likely to take one again. Add to this the fact that many of these pike had avoided capture years ago when the culling was carried out and dare I suggest the older a pike gets the more cautious it can become. I have to qualify this of course by saying that any pike no matter how old and experienced can have an "off" day and get caught!

to be a major problem. My plan was to leap frog around the lake and in so doing put a bait in front of most if not all of the big pike I thought were present. About 10.30 Tony Bridgefoot went by on the other side of the lake walking around. As he did so I had a run on the jack pike and by the time he got around to me the pike was on the mat ready to be weighed. He helped me weigh the fish and photograph it. At first I was ecstatic because I thought I had caught the fish that had weighed 29-12 previously. If this one had increased a pound in weight what was last seasons 38 pounder going to be?

When Steve Broad of Angling Times compared the photographs he informed me that the 30-12 was the big fish. The fish was caught in February 12 months after I caught her and weighed 22lb. All in all a sad end for a fabulous fish. With the realisation that all the big pike were one fish it brought home the reality that I would not have another big fish to target in the next few months.

31-04 Hardwick

Hardwick Lake is one of Len Gurd's Linear Oxford Fisheries. All are mature gravel pits stocked with a variety of species with the emphasis on carp. The fact that there are quality roach, bream and tench present means that it is capable of producing the odd big pike. Hardwick is about 20 acres in size and Roy Parsons the baliff had told me that there didn't seem to be many pike present. It had previously produced pike to 27-12 this was 12 months before I fished it. At the time I was fishing the other pits on the complex which had a much better head of twenty pounders. I kept driving past Hardwick thinking that one day I'd have a go on there.

I had initially planned to fish Guys Lake, but there were too many carp anglers on it. So I went to Hardwick and had my first session there. Within an hour I had caught a 16 pounder which looked like a trout fed pike. By the looks of this fish Roy Parsons's assessment seemed correct. Plenty of food and very few pike, always a recipe for a big one. Before the end of the 2000/2001 season I had caught a couple of twenty pounders from the water and decided the next season I would pay it more attention. Unfortunately very soon after starting my 2002 campaign I pulled out of a very large fish. Twenty minutes earlier I had landed a 25 pounder so I think it would be fair to say I was in a good position to know what a good fish felt like. I also saw the fish briefly about 5 yards out before it rolled over and spat the bait out.

It wasn't to be until 12 months later that my efforts on the water were rewarded. As is so often the case when you catch a big pike you wonder at how easy it seemed. Of course in reality in the moment of celebration you tend to forget all the blank sessions which led up to the capture. She took a large livebait, something which other pike anglers had probably not tried on the water. Also I had drifted the bait out 120 yards to an area which had probably not been fished by anyone else. The area I was fishing was fairly featureless, what I was relying on was the fact that any big pike in this water was used to eating large preyfish. This is typical of many gravel pits where small fish are

31-04 Hardwick

scarce. This may be a simple formulae, but some pike anglers seem to discount the obvious. Perhaps they think too much about what they are doing. The state of the moon is not going to help unless you have the right bait within, sight, sound or smell of a big pike.

I had tried myself all the obvious dodges such as night fishing, but that had not worked at all. In the end the run I wanted came at 1pm and within a few minutes I had a big, long gravel pit pike in the net. Hardwick is one of the few places I still go back to. It is simply because there is the element of the unknown about the place. It might just grow a really big pike. Every other fish species grows big in Hardwick and a pit only up the road did a 35-12 a few years ago.

33-12 Ladybower

This was to be our last year of exclusive fishing on Ladybower. We arrived for our first two day session just after the trout season had ended in mid November. We headed for the Snake Arm and though we had a good day Neville took the honours with a 31-10 and a 25lb plus two other twenties. I trailed in his wake with two of 23-00 and 20-02. The next day rather than return to the same area and probably struggle we headed for Fairholmes and a bit of bank fishing off the car park. Things started slowly and Neville had the first good fish, but it swam into a sunken tree and broke the trace. We both had the usual two paternostered livebaits each out in the area and it was one of mine which went next. That was a 25-08. Then things went rather quiet, but from time to time I had a few casts with a lure. At first I was using a Springdawg when a big fat fish came after it. It was so keen to have it that it stuck its head out of the water trying to grab it. Try as I might I couldn't get it to take. So I tried the Mister Muskie spoon and it had a go at that as well and missed it!

Late in the afternoon I sneaked off to have a go where the river came in. Again I was casting with the Springdawg and after half a dozen casts something took as soon as I started winding. I didn't really think it was that big and landing it was always going be by hand because the net was back with Neville at the car park. I shouted to him to bring the scales and thought it looked about 28lb. Only when we weighed it did he realise that it was lots bigger than that. It was an incredibly fat fish and weighed 33-12. Was it the fish that had followed me earlier and had moved to the other swim? It probably was because there was one big fish around that day which had up to then not been caught. Having followed twice earlier, by the end of the day it was probably just that little bit more determined to grab a lure. I had already taken two other thirties from that swim as it got dark so perhaps I had spotted a pattern there.

31-08 Ladybower

This was the last 30lb plus pike I was to catch from Ladybower, unless of course I'm lucky enough to catch one on the organised pike fishing dates. So far I've managed one twenty pounder and a hangover. January had always been a good month on Ladybower possibly because trout stocks had reached their lowest levels. Also February always

33-12 Ladybower

something to the top which then decided that was not where it wanted to be and it powered off back downstream. With the flow to help it, it really did fight hard. The gap in the reeds I was fishing from was fairly tight with reeds standing out in the water. I had to be careful to make sure it didn't kite into those and likewise netting a big fish in running water and a gale is always a risky situation. As it approached the net I could see it was a monster, a view I enjoyed a lot more when it was safely in the net.

It had to be the big one and as to what it weighed, well all sorts of ideas go through your head. Had it just eaten a 3lb bream or had it not eaten since its last capture? Either way it didn't take long to find out. It is rare for me to get the shakes, but this time shake I did. I had to brace the scales with a bank stick to get a steady reading which settled out at 38-04. I then sacked her and phoned Angling Times. Luckily Mick Rouse was in and together with Steve Broad and Dave Woodmansey they came down to do the photographs. While I waited I phoned Neville and said. "You know that Mammoth Pike book?" "Well save a space in it" His reply was along the lines of "Oh no what have you done now" I duly told him and asked if he was going to congratulate me. He said yes "congratulations, you are a bloody nuisance" Shortly after I had another low double and stayed the night. I had one run in the night which mauled the bait, but nothing more by dawn. At about 8am I decided to go and have a look around fishing other stretches of the drain. By then though the wind had dropped totally and everywhere seemed totally dead. The day before had been the time to fish and as luck would have it my path and a particularly interesting fish had crossed. The reason that pike had got so big was a combination of factors. Salt water had wiped out most of the pike in the late eighties and those few that survived probably grew very well. The drain had never really been on the circuit of well known pike fishing waters and because of this the pike had the advantage of growing relatively undisturbed. Also unusual for a fen drain the drain had a larger stock of smallish common carp which would make a very good meal for any big pike. I do not spend much time thinking about records, but it is interesting to note that that fish is the biggest, second biggest, third, fourth and fifth biggest Fenland pike on record. A very special fish.

32-02 Wintons

Wintons Fishery is a well known commercial fishery near Burgess Hill in West Sussex. Owner Alan Hetherington created these waters from scratch. They are heavily stocked with all manner of species including some huge catfish to 60lbs, 40lb plus carp zander and some pike. It is unclear what purpose the pike serve because in most commercial fisheries the owners remove pike if they find their way into their water. As is typical of most commercial fisheries the water is very coloured which again is suprising because we do not generally think of pike thriving in muddy water. There are three small pools on the site, Mallard, Kingfisher and Heron. Wintons has produced the odd big pike in the past, but few people really considered it worth asking Alan if they could fish for them

I had first visited the fishery a few years ago for a couple of day's catfishing; I did quite well with fish of 40lb 6oz and 36-08. I then returned about five years later and caught

32-04 Wintons Heron Lake

a 61-04 catfish. At the time Alan told me about the 32lb pike that was in Kingfisher Lake. I went down once in the winter to fish for it, but the lake was frozen over so that was that. Two years later having heard that there were now more than just a 32 pounder to be caught I thought I'd ask Alan if I could fish it again. He gave me 24hrs and I could only fish under strict conditions. These were that I used a single hook and no wire trace. He was concerned about potential damage to the catfish by people fishing with conventional pike terminal tackle.

I started off on Kingfisher Lake the home of the original 32 pounder which had since died. I had a few hours on there which resulted in a 12 pounder followed by a 20-04. I was fishing with a sardine using a size 1 single hook to Supatress. This wire has copper fibres running through it. It had previously proved to be pike proof on another water. I then moved onto Heron Lake and had a jack. I then added a 24-12 having fished all the way around the lake. While in the last swim to be fished I spotted a big fish roll presumably a pike fry feeding. I only had 45 minutes of daylight so I decided to move back to where I had seen the pike roll. I set up my bivvy for the night, put three fresh baits on and had a run straight away on one rod which was about 8lb. Then nothing happened until quarter to four in the morning. The transmitter in my bivvy was bleeping and the red LED told me that it was the bait in the swim where I had seen the pike roll. I struck into the fish, feeling a big fish. It only took a few minutes to land and once in the net the head torch revealed that it was a thirty pounder. She weighed 32-04. Soon my twenty four hours were up and it was time to move to the River Adur which was not productive. Just to prove I'm not always lucky I was standing on the bridge when I saw a pike of at least 15lb roll. Rushing to get my rods I put my bib and braces on leaving the braces hanging down. I put one boot on and then stepped back not realising that I'd just pushed the braces into a great big pile of doggy poo. I then pulled the straps over my shoulder and thought; "Where's that horrible smell coming from". I soon realised it was me and I had to partially undress and wash the filth off in the river. I had to fish for about 5 hours without half my clothes. Soon the M25 looked more inviting than shivering and blanking so I went home.

41-04 Sussex Lake

While browsing through Neville's book Mammoth Pike I spotted a fish from Surrey or Sussex that had turned up a couple of times early in 2004. Now any fish which gets caught a couple of times in succession is a fish which likes eating. On that basis such a fish was probably catchable, simply because it couldn't keep its mouth shut. The first problem though was to find out exactly where it came from. Richard Howard, features editor of Anglers Mail mentioned the fish had come out again at the end of 2004. So this fish was clearly getting caught on a fairly regular basis which is always a plus point for someone like me who has limited time to target an individual fish. A few weeks went by and Gary Banks just happened to have a conversation with Richard Howard and he wondered why I had not had a go for the fish. The main reason for this was simple; I still didn't know where it lived! This problem was soon solved when Richard told Gary the location of the nearest small town to the water. Gary then simply finished the task,

41-04 Sussex Lake

by ringing round the local tackle shops. Initially this was without success, but as luck would have it a gun shop came up with the name of the water.

So one Sunday much to the annoyance of Diane my long suffering wife, Gary persuaded me to join him for a run down to the lake to confirm his deductions. Sure enough when we arrived it had to be the lake, just looking at the surrounding woodlands. We fished for a few hours without anything to show for our efforts. Then the man who owned the lake came around to see us. He told us it was £12 each to fish with three rods. I gave him £30 for the two of us and he gave me a pound change. As he gave me the pound he said "My names Robin". Gary promptly replied "Robin by name, Robin by nature." He promptly burst out laughing, realised his mistake and gave me the right change. He gave me his phone number and we headed back to Wolverhampton. All in all a 350 mile round trip for a dabble and a chat.

My interest by now was aroused so the time had come to plan an attempt to catch this fish which most likely would weigh anything between 35 and 38lbs. The plan was to go for a two day trip the next week. I rang Robin on Monday and the big fish had not been out, so the Trooper was loaded up and ready to go. At 3.15am on the Tuesday morning I was on the road and introduced myself once more to the "joys" of the M25. I arrived at about 6am, waited until 6.30am ready to be first on the lake. I picked a swim based on the idea that I'd be able to cover as much of the lake as possible from the one spot. I asked Robin if I could stop on the lake to save me packing all my gear away and he O.K. ed this. In this way I had secured the swim I needed. The first day produced just the one double on a deadbait. For one heart stopping moment the way the fish was running I was convinced it was to be one run wham bam thank you mamm. I was wrong though. The next day the temperature had gone up one or two degrees and I thought I'd be in with a chance that day, but nothing at all happened. This was a big disappointment. Now I had forgotten to take my mobile phone so it was a struggle keeping in touch with home, but luckily Robin let me use his phone a couple of times. However the curse of the Williams was about to strike. As I walked up his drive two fire engines arrived. His chimney was on fire. The fireman quickly dealt with the problem and soon I was having a beer with him laughing about the near disaster. I then phoned Diane to tell her for the first time in at least 20 years that I was staying an extra night. I just had a feeling that something might happen because the air temperature was due to rise as high as 15C the next day. Interestingly Robin asked me if I thought that his fish would reach 40lbs. I quickly told him that I didn't think it had a chance. This just goes to show that even I get things totally wrong from time to time. On this water you are allowed to fish from 6.30am so I cast my three rods out and within ten minutes I had a run. It was the float legered herring that was trundling off. A quick strike and then everything happened very quickly. The fish came quickly to the net. I couldn't see exactly how big it was, but luckily it swam straight over the net and she was mine. I put the rod down and then I looked in the net. It was the lifting part that astounded me because it was a job to manhandle it up the bank. I realised by then that I had my target fish there on the unhooking mat. What surprised me was how fat it was. It looked almost as if it was going to burst. I couldn't believe how deep it looked on the mat. The only way to find out how big it really was was to get on with the weighing. Unhooking was straight forward with one hook in the scissors and the other hanging loose. As I unhooked it I noticed something sticking out of her throat. It looked to me to be the tail of a tench, possible around the 2 to 3lb mark. I weighed her without extra support and it went over 41lb. No-one was more surprised that I was so I used a bank stick to enable me to get better support of the scales. This time the scales settled at 41-04.

I put the fish in a tube in deep water and sat back and tried to compose myself and cooked some breakfast. In about 10 minutes another pike angler arrived on the bank and he spoke to me asking if I was Nige Williams and if I'd done any good. In actual fact I think he said "Oh no is it Nige Williams?". My reply probably made him feel even worse when I said I'd just caught a forty pounder. I asked him if he'd photograph it and he was curious as to whether it was the 38-08 he had weighed and photographed for another angler ten days previously. He explained that Dave Gawthorne had caught it on the 29th December and the other chap had had it on the 8th of January. I had caught it on the 20th January and with this you could see that she was roughly coming out every 10 to 12 days. As daylight began to break we got the fish out of the tube and while I was getting the camera sorted out I noticed he was having a look down its throat to see what was inside it.

He was good enough to take the pictures and the fish was strong enough to soak me as it powered off. With that there was no longer any point in staying. I needed to get some Brownie points with the wife so I decided to set off home. Just before then Robin arrive and when I told him about the fish he burst out laughing and said you deserved it for staying the extra day. He asked me which fish it was and suddenly it dawned on me that there might be two big fish in there. He went and fetched two photographs of two different fish caught only a few days apart. One was 32-08 the other was 35-04. The 32-08 looked a longer fish than the big one, but I was not sure which fish I had actually had. Was it the Gawthorne fish or the other one suitable padded out by all the deadbaits which pike anglers had been discarding? It wasn't until I had the pictures processed that I was able to see that it was the Gawthorne fish.

Luck had been with me again. It is one thing to put yourself in the right place at the right time. It is another thing and something which no-one has any control of, to catch a fish after it had been on a feeding binge which had probably terrorised all the other inhabitants of the lake the week before. There lays the problem, facing any angler targeting a known fish. A thirty pounder which has not fed for a week could weigh 29lbs. The same fish with an appetite could weigh 32lbs. So if you are not as lucky as I was consider this; the same fish at 35lbs would be more enough to make any angler blissfully happy. Even it weighed 34lb no sane person would complain. There has to be some perspective applied to the weights of pike, otherwise there is the risk of being disappointed with the capture of a fish because it isn't big enough. If you start thinking like that I suggest you are not going to be pike fishing for much longer.

41-04 showing how fat it was

AN OVERVIEW

Reading about the captures of my thirty pounders readers might be excused for thinking that I'm only interested in fish of this size. That would be a mistake. I have much lower targets for my everyday fishing. Twenty pounders are an obvious target, but even on the best waters they do not turn up to order. While I do not focus my attention on waters which produce lots of twenty pounders and no bigger fish, I still appreciate the fish which turn up when I'm after a monster. I certainly do not throw a 21 pounder back in disgust because it wasn't the target fish. To become so focussed risks losing a total grip of piking reality. In the next section I'll relate my experiences on a number of waters. Not all have seen me walk off with instant success. Indeed some waters have defeated me completely.

A lot of trips end up with a blank or worse. In October of 2004 I was giving a talk up on Teeside and I was keen to find somewhere local to fish. A look at the map revealed one likely venue up in the Pennines. I decided to organise a two day trip around the talk which was a mere 460 mile round trip from my house. The weather needed to be right for this venue because it was right up in the hills and in a very exposed location. The forecast was dry with light winds, but when John Simcox and I arrived just before 7am it was raining. The brollys were soon erected and the rods cast out.

At 10.30am I had my first run, a 21-04oz pike, a bonus except for its condition. On both flanks were sizeable round sores. It looked like it had been wedged somewhere and had got damaged struggling to escape. A quick photo and she swam away just fine. By now the rain was getting heavier and streams and waterfalls nearby were pouring into the fishery. We decided to move our rods a couple of metres up the bank.

At about 5pm I had to leave John, he was about to erect the bivvy while I went to my slide show. Jokingly, I told him to pitch up a further 15 metres further up the bank - so we weren't 'swept away.'

Five miles into my journey to Teeside and the weather had cleared up, and I was looking forward to the next days piking. The evening at Darlington/Teeside PAC went well and I set off to return to the lake around 10.45pm. The weather had changed drastically and fog had descended so thickly I could hardly see to drive back. I ended up getting lost and the journey back took me nearly three times as long as it should have done. When I got there I was knackered and was desperate to get into my sleeping bag for a kip, and I told John the water level couldn't possibly come any higher. Famous last words.

Sleep at last, but not for long. It started hammering down, and the wind got stronger and stronger. An hour later we were in a pool of water with waves lashing against the front of the bivvy; I couldn't believe how quickly the level was rising. The whole bivvy then collapsed on top of us!

The first day was spent sorting the gear and the boats out. The house we were in had three rooms, but we had to give one of them to Neil because he snored so badly. No-one could survive a night in a room with Neil, not unless they were deaf or equipped with ear protectors! Duncan shared with Neville, Neil was on his own and I had to share with Nige and Kev. I was piggy in the middle with Kev snoring fit to bring the rafters down. Little wonder that I didn't get much sleep that week!

Our first morning dawned very nicely indeed, very little wind and sunny. We all headed off to the Ferry Bridge to launch our boats. Nige and I were in a 16 ft Bonwitcho, Neville and Duncan in Tango and Neil and Kev in a Lough boat. We all motored around to Maamtrasna Bay and we fished without result for a couple of hours. The weather had been steadily deteriorating so the other four decided to head back. Nige and I on the other hand decided to stop a bit longer. Our bit longer only lasted about 15 minutes as it was clear that the weather conditions were no longer a joke. As we headed back we came across Kev and Neil waving franticly. They had run out of petrol! Nige volunteered to tow them back to the Ferry Bridge. Kev tried to remonstrate telling us that it was really rough in the main Lough. He had no interest in going out there. However ever confident Nige wasn't having any of that. He was sure he could tow Kev and Nige back with no trouble. So off we set towing a 19ft Lough boat behind us and it soon became clear that this was a big mistake and I mean big with a capital B! The waves on the main lake were unbelievable and towing a boat behind us which constantly jerked the tow rope was making it very difficult for us to progress. However we couldn't turn back. Once you are heading into a big wave you have to keep going unless you own a very big boat. I remember looking back at big Kev and to me he was holding on for dear life though if asked today he would probably deny it. It was certainly the scariest experience I have ever had. As we struggled on Nige asked me where my lifejacket was. I said that it was back in the car, not really the best decision I had made that week! However we made it back where Neville was waiting for us. All of us were well and truly shook up and didn't want to experience that again. We all thought that the weather couldn't get any worse than that, but we were wrong. The wind blew every day and fishing from the boats was impossible. We did try bank fishing, but you are so restricted compared to fishing from a boat. Also the strong winds were churning almost all the areas we could bank fish into a brown mess. In the end most of the week was spent in the pubs teaching the locals to play pool and driving around looking for new spots. During the week Nige went a bit fast through a deep puddle in his Isuzu Trooper and it promptly expired. Now though Nige was in the AA, he didn't have full European cover. Kev then in his brand new Discovery towed Nige to McDonalds motors in Ballinrobe. We told the mechanic what had happened and he said "No problem, I'll sort it out". Next day we returned to find Nige's fuel pump in bits on the front seat. Out came the mechanic who said he couldn't fix it and then tried to charge him for it. After a few words we agreed to pay him £50 just to get the truck back. Kev then towed him back to our digs. There was only one option to get the AA to recover the vehicle to the UK, but he had to pay for that which didn't please him too much!

Even when the weather is really bad. There are always smaller waters to have a go on. They do not offer the potential of the really big waters, but when you are a long way from home on a fishing trip, you have to fish somewhere. We decided to try Ross Lake a fairly large water to the West of Lough Corrib. Unfortunately the lake was in flood and didn't look very good. Our initial doubts were well founded as we had no action at all. Such was the level of excitement that Kev backed his Discovery down to the water and gave it a wash. This was a mistake because the day ended with a water fight. (now, now kids).

Next morning we decided to change boat partners and I drew the short straw and ended up with Kev. Kev and I took the Bonwitcho and shot down upper Mask to fish where I had lost those fish the previous trip. Almost straight away Kev had a run on a mackerel. He wound down and struck the fish coming straight to the surface where it shook the hooks free. Kev was gutted as the fish looked about 20lb.

As the middle of the day came we heard a boat come roaring up the Lough. It was a rib and we thought it was going to go straight past us. Instead it veered sharp left and came straight over to us. It turned out to be the Western Region Fisheries Board. They checked all our gear and even made us wind in so we could check that we were not livebaiting. Once they had dealt with us they went over to Duncan and Neil and then Neville and Nige, but they were wasting their time because the others were behaving themselves impeccably. Later that day as we packed up Kev managed to let go of Nige's new anchor rope. We spent the next half and hour chucking spoons around trying to snag the rope. Eventually Kev hooked the rope and got the anchor back. (That was all he did catch!)

The rest of the week was hopeless because of the weather so on the last night we decided to get bladdered and bladdered we got. The next morning we had to get the boats out and my head was pounding. I swore never to drink again.... Now I had sold my Bonwitcho to Neville and we were recovering it from the Ferry Bridge. We pulled it out and parked it out of the way higher up the slipway. Neville then fetched out a wad of notes and paid me for the boat. I said thanks and just then a huge gust of wind hit us. The cabin on the Bonwitcho was torn off and went straight over our heads and the road landing in the bushes. I quickly pushed that money a bit deeper into my pocket. Neville's face was a picture and I think in the end he saw the funny side. So ended another trip, but this time there was to be no return trip. The gill nets returned and that signalled the destruction of some of the finest pike fishing in Europe. Until the gill netting ceases I do not suppose we will ever return to that most beautiful waters, Lough Mask.

LOUGH ALLEN

After our previous years disaster on Lough Mask and the re-introduction of the gill nets Gary and I suggested to Neville that rather giving up the trips to Ireland he organise one to Lough Allen. This is a water Neville had had some success on in the past and of

Dusk is sometimes the best time for a big pike

course there were more pike there to be caught than on Mask. A spring trip was organised and I'll let Gary Banks tell the story of this trip which worked out quite well for most of us.

This trip saw most of the usual crew, Nige, I, Neil, Duncan and Neville. Kev couldn't make it because of work commitments and his place was taken by Ian Greenacre from Norfolk. Neville had booked the O'Dwyers by the side of the lake. Alas Ros was eventually forced to sell up due to little Ros having MS and needing a lot of extra care. That sadly was all in the future.

We arrived on the Saturday and were soon itching to get out on the lake. Nige and I headed off towards some islands in the south where some friends of ours had caught fish to 29lbs the previous year. We reached our chosen spot and I must admit it looked pikey. Unfortunately all the optimism proved to be unfounded. On return to the house we found that no-one had any action to report so we headed for the pub to acquaint ourselves with the locals and the Guinness, not necessarily in that order!

The usual plan when fishing waters such as Lough Allen is to move around and never fish the same area the next day. With this in mind we headed for the North end of the lake to fish the North Bay. This is a large bay connected to the main lake by a narrow channel. Once inside the bay it looked absolutely gorgeous. We all opted to bank fish and because the weather was really nice it was one of those few occasions in Ireland when it was possible to take in the sun while watching the rods. All we needed now were a few decent pike, but for most of us these were hard to find with only a few jacks caught. Except of course for Mr Williams who had a nice 15 pounder. The long journey home ended with most of us heading into town again to the nearest bar.

The beauty of a wild water, Lough Allen in spring

Next morning we woke up to rain, lots of glorious rain. After having enjoyed some nice weather we were really looking forward to getting soaked! Anyway we didn't let this dampen our spirits (excuse the pun). We headed off to fish Rhoss Du Bay a very famous spot where lots of big fish had been caught in the past. We arrived to find no-one else there which was very good news. We anchored up and cast out two livebaits and one deadbait each around the boat. Now Nige's cuddy isn't very big and it was a tight squeeze with two great big hairy blokes trying to keep out of the rain and cook breakfast. Then out of the blue we heard one of the multipliers scream. We both tried to get out of the door together with the inevitable Chaplinesque result. Youth however prevailed and I got out first. It was my rod and the bait was a mackerel. I wound down and bent into a decent pike. She didn't take long to land and weighed about 13lb. She was quickly unhooked and returned. This was the highlight of the day apart from Nige needing to lighten his load in a bucket, but I'll draw a veil over these unsavoury events. The usual evening routine was followed to the T. When Nige and I go away for a week we treat it as a holidays and certainly have no intention of fishing at the levels of intensity we normally operate too.

My Wilson Flyer moored at Arden on Loch Lomond

Next morning the weather had brightened up considerably. Today we were going to fish Balmaha probably the hardest fished area on the whole Loch. We caught quite a few fish that morning in several different areas, but nothing huge. Balmaha can produce in a variety of areas. The drop off of the Endrick Bank is probably the most popular pike fishing area; however it continues to produce inspite of the pressure. Sometimes Cro-Min bay is where you need to be. Other times the Endrick River can be well worth a look. These pike move around a lot and the angler has got to be prepared to find where the fish have gone too.

We could see another boat along the drop off, it too being a Wilson flyer. It proved to be Brian Ingrams, one of only a handful of people to have had a 40 pounder from Llandegfedd. He was fishing with Dave Skudder, both of them being fairly regular visitors to the Loch... We went over to have a chat and arranged to meet them in the pub that night. Brian told us to try Slate Bay as some good fish had come out of there earlier in the year. So the next day it had to be Slate Bay. In the meantime some more beer had to be consumed. I suspect readers have by now come to the conclusion that we are all alcoholics. I'sh denysh sthat! That night we left Brian and Dave in the pub intent on getting up early the next day.

Slate Bay simply screams pike, it is surrounded by trees and reeds and we arrived early intent on extracting some of its pike. However it wasn't until midday that my multiplier started to click. Something had grabbed my paternostered roach livebait. It wasn't a huge fishy at 16-08, but at the time it was my Lomond personal best. So I was pleased and my view is that pike fishing is like taking steps. You try and ascend each step one at a time and each time you make a step you gain a little more satisfaction. Only the very lucky and Nige can jump the whole staircase in one go. Unfortunately on that day we didn't catch anymore fish. One of the problems with a well fished water is that all the popular areas are fished fairly regularly. This means that large numbers of big pike never get the chance to accumulate in these areas. Because we were relative novices on the water we had not had time to learn of some of the more out of the way big pike spots.

We carried on that week fishing areas such as Portnellan, but nothing bigger than low doubles turned up. The problem with having a week away on a hard fished water is that you could easily miss the one week when they were really on. In an ideal world you would have a mate who could let you know when the pike were on and then you would drop everything and head to the water. Unfortunately such helpful people are thin on the ground and anyway getting time off work at short notice is not always easy.

CATFISH

Like many people I started fishing for catfish in the eighties. In those days the number of venues available was limited. The most famous of all of them was Claydon Lake. You would look at the place and think "This is a glorified farm pond"! Lots of people were fishing there and to add to your problems there was no night fishing. We all had to sleep in our cars and then at dawn it was a race across the fields to grab a swim. On my first visit I had only been there half an hour before I had my first cat a fish of 22-12. I gave it about another half a dozen goes and had one more of 20-09. It was at the time when they were coming out on sea deadbaits. Mackerel heads and sardines were the favoured baits, the mackerel having the advantage that the carp couldn't suck the baits to death. It was all free lining in those days.

My first big catfish from Claydon in 1982 (22-12)

I used to soak my hook length of quicksilver in oil which I think helped me to be more successful. After then there wasn't much catfishing about which interested me until Wintons came on the scene. On my first visit I had a 40-06 and a 36-08 which at the time was one of the biggest braces of catfish caught in the UK. Two weeks later I returned, but did no good at all. The Wintons fish were caught on livebaits fished on the surface. Then I had a go on one of Rob Hale's waters and had a 32-08 from there. Tackle was 12ft 3lb test rods and braid had by then come into use. The livebaits were hooked through the tail with a John Roberts bait saver or piece of elastic band to make sure they didn't get off. The cats would come right up to the surface to grab them, even in 15 feet of water. Then Shatterford became interesting as a catfish water. First trip produced a 27, two weeks later Ross had a 27. A few years later I went back and had a 39-04 and a 35. Ross had a 32. Just after that I had a night and a day on Bluebell. Ross had a 30lb 9oz.

In 2001 I returned to Wintons and by now they had got to 60lb plus. Ross I and went down for a couple of days. The weather was really hot and the first day was uneventful. Ross wanted to wander off and have a talk with someone who was on the water. I told him not to as he was supposed to have the first run. About ten minutes after he had gone off somewhere at 11a.m. there was a huge swirl by one livebait, but it missed it. Whatever it was it had another go and this time it took the bait. It weighed 61-04, 12oz short of the record. I had to get the owner to help me weigh it because it was too big for my scales and my sling. A couple of weeks later we went down again because Ross was moaning at me and he had a 36-08 at night. We actually caught our livebaits while we were there the baits being about 4oz. They were usually roach or skimmers.

Just a catfish, but at 61-04 my biggest fish of any description

One of my last catfish trips was to Swangey after I had, had the 33lb pike. Again fishing the surface catfish rig I had a really small kitten and a 4-15 eel. Both were caught 20 foot off of the bottom. Other big eels that have turned up included a 6-01 and a 4-12 from Docklow Pools. We were going eel fishing on the Rabbit Run, but when we got there it had all been fenced off. Des was with me and he rang Mike at Docklow and he agreed that we could have a night there. My first fish was 6-01 followed by the 4-12 on legered gudgeon deadbaits. The head was ripped off and a size 1 hook inserted through the tail root. I always had the feeling that catching big eels invariably killed them. The 6 was mouth hooked and as far as I know survived, but a later trip to Linear fisheries college lake ledgering worms at long range saw a half a dozen eels between 3-14 and 3-15 all pumping blood on landing and none survived.

Jason Davis had some catfish in one of his lakes that he wanted moving. We went over to have a go. The first night I had a big fish on that I pulled out of. The next night on the same rig as I was using Jason had a 44 pounder. I didn't actually catch anything from there of note, only a few kittens.

A chance visit to Docklow Pool resulted in this 6-01 eel

DOING A FAVOUR

The very nature of the weekly angling press means that there always has to be something new to report. Angling Times came up with the idea of getting the editor Richard Lee to catch a 20lb pike. Martin Bowler had been tasked with this job and soon realised it wasn't the same as catching a big carp, barbel or chub. His first thought was to head for Linear Fisheries at Oxford. After all many of these pits have produced twenty pound plus pike, sometimes bigger. However they are hard waters and there was no guarantee of success in the two days they had allocated to the project. Indeed the first day yielded just one small pike. They intended to carry on fishing the same pit the next day and by lunch just one more small fish had graced their net.

I just happened to be filming with Sky on a nearby pit and Martin rang me and asked if I had any ideas. Jokingly I suggested he needed a man to catch a man's fish! It's a good job he's a mate! I joined them later, but they had made no progress so I told them to pack up, we were on the move. It was a bit of a trek and I'm sure I had them totally lost by the time we got there. I encouraged Richard to get cast out quickly and soon three deadbaits were cast out into an area where I had caught a 27 pounder a month of so earlier. A short while later one of his indicators dropped off and as easy as that Richard hooked and landed a superb pike of 26-02. If it all sounds too easy there is probably a logical explanation for what happened. A lot of pits in the Oxford area have had their prey fish stocks denuded by cormorants. Richard's fish had probably been a lot bigger before. Now with food hard to find this fish was a sucker for a free meal. Sadly pike like this can eventually lose condition and eventually starve. Sometimes the best thing you can do for fish like this is empty the contents of your freezer into their pit. Who knows a bit of extra food could make life easier for the old girl.

Richard Lee with his 26 pounder

FEN ZANDER

In 1989 I started to get interested in zander. I started on Coombe Abbey which is fairly near to me, at least compared to the Fens. I had fish there to 6-06 during a couple of night sessions. I then went to have a look at the Cut Off and early sessions there produced fish to 7-14 and 7-15. Then I stumbled on the Middle Level and a chap who I took with me Robbie Harrison had a 10-02 and that started to get me really interested.

A 13-02 zander from the Middle Level

My best zander so far, a 14-14 from Middle Level

I decided to team up with Dave Phillips a local angler with an extensive knowledge of Fen zander. The arrival of October saw our initial foray together and I was glad that I had the company of Dave because the usual problem associated with Fen drains immediately struck me. Where to start? A shared effort, at least in theory, should help narrow the odds in our favour. There was just one problem: the pike had not heard that we were zander fishing. So after lots of pike action I went home wondering what had happened there!

Over the next few weeks the weather took a turn for the worse and I didn't get down until November of 1989. It was a two day session. I dropped in by a bridge, a supposedly good swim and set up in the dark. The night got colder and wetter and more miserable. With nothing to show for the effort, at dawn I moved swims. It took twenty minutes to move and eventually I found a spot I fancied. The plan was to give this spot an hour and then leap frog back along the drain. I didn't have an hour though because the alarm sounded, but whatever it was dropped the bait. I recast and thirty minutes later the performance was repeated. I recast again and this time third time lucky the alarm sounded and this time line was running out. Up went the rod into whatever it was. I suspected a pike, but soon I saw the characteristic golden flash typical of a zander. I took special care landing this one because it was my first zander from the water. Once in the net I threw the rod up the bank and scrambled up the bank with my prize. Once on the scales she pulled them around to 11-01. I could not have been more thrilled.

I recast and promptly dropped a good fish off. Somewhat fed up I recast, but it all ended well because I had yet another run and this one was even bigger than the first one. It looked huge in the water and in those days it was a big, big zander. Once in the net I realised I was shaking like a leaf. Something that doesn't happen that often. She weighed 14-14 and is still my best zander.

A few small pike followed by a few 7 pounders. I didn't get chance to go back until the end of the season and I had a 13-06 and a 7-15. Tactics were legered eel sections on two rods and paternostered livebaits on a free running paternoster. The baits were good sized roach and dace fished on 2lb 12ft Armalites, 12lb mono and size 6 trebles to 20lb Drennan wire. A couple of years later I had a 12 pounder from the Level, but by then I was starting to look at the River Severn. I fished at Upton upon Severn and had fish to 11 pounds with a couple of other doubles. The swims to look for were slack slow areas and the mouth of the marina.

NIGE'S PIKE OVER 25lb

41-04	Sussex Lake.	2005
40-12	Bluebell Lake.	1996
39-08	Bough Beech.	1992
38-04	Fen Drain	2004
33-14	Swangey Pit.	1998
33-13	Ladybower.	2000
33-12	Ladybower.	2002
32-08	Derravaragh.	1995
32-06	Blithfield Reservoir.	2002
32-04	Wintons Heron Lake.	2004
32-02	Belvide Reservoir.	1984
31-10	Ladybower.	2002
31-08	Hampshire Avon.	1996?
31-08	Ladybower.	2003
31-08	Ladybower.	2001
31-04	Hardwick.	2002
30-12	Belvide Reservoirs.	1984
30-12	Bluebell Kingfisher Lake.	2002
30-12	Ladybower.	2001
30-09	Tong Mere.	1984
30-08	River Adur.	1996
28-02	Tong Mere.	
27-12	Fen Drain.	
27-10	Abingdon Pit 2	2004
27-08	Lough Allen.	
27-08	Lakeside.	
27-06	Ladybower.	2001
27-04	Ringstead.	
26-10	Belvide Reservoir.	
26-10	Ladybower.	2002
26-08	Ladybower.	2002
26-08	Hampshire Avon.	
26-04	Abingdon Pit 1.	2004
26-04	Ladybower.	2003
26-02	Ladybower.	2002
25-10	Blithfield.	2004
25-10	Tong Mere.	

25-08	Ladybower.	2002
25-08	Hardwick.	
25-04	Staunton Harold.	
25-04	Ringstead.	
25-04	North Level.	
25-02	Bough Beech.	
25-02	Ladybower.	
25-02	Smiths.	2002
25-02	Anglesey.	2005

TOTAL 46

EARLY DAYS

Everyone remembers their first twenty pound pike much as we all remember our first kiss or for some people their first run in with the law! My first twenty pound plus pike came in 1981 from Lady Barbaras Pool at Patshull and fell to a legered mackerel. It had been a fairly long journey to that first really big fish. I've no idea really why we equate 20lbs with a specimen weight, but that's the way it is. Though 19-15 is almost twenty pounds, isn't it? That particular fish weighed 23-10 and the suddenly rise to prominence of Patshull came after they had started to stock it with trout. Unfortunately in those days the pike had a very uncertain life expectancy if left where they were so I was moving these fish to Belvide. There was one fish I moved that didn't get weighed by myself which was said to have weighed 22lb. However when the photographs came out my fellow Severn Valley Specimen Group members derided it to such as extent that I never counted it.

BEST FISH FROM VENUES & No. OF TWENTIES FROM EACH

Abingdon Pit 1	26-04	1
Abingdon Pit 2	27-02	1
Anglesey Lake	25-02	2
Aqualite Mere	22-12	4
Blithfield Reservoir	32-06	3
Bluebell Lake	40-12	1
Bough Beech	39-08	2
Chew Reservoir	21-04	2
Cut Off Channel	23-12	6
Derravaragh	32-08	4
Fen Drain	38-04	2
Gailey Reservoir	23-10	6
Grafham Reservoir	21-00	1
Guys Lake	21-02	1
Hardwick Lake	31-04	6
Hampshire Avon	31-08	2
Kingfisher Lake	30-12	1
Ladybower Reservoir	33-14	29
Lake Windermere	22-01	2
Lakeside Essex	27-08	2
Llandegfedd Reservoir	21-08	1
Llangorse Lake	24-04	5
Lough Allen	27-08	1
Lough Derg	22-14	4
Mill Lake	23-14	2
North Level	25-04	1

Nunnery D Lake	24-04	2
Nunnery E Lake	21-12	1
Over Water	20-08	1
Patshull Church Pool	22-12	3
Patshull Great Lake	22-12	1
Patshull Upper Church	23-10	1
Rabbit Run	22-14	7
Ringstead Lake	27-04	2
River Adur	30-08	1
River Severn	22-14	3
River Thurne	22-06	1
River Wye	23-08	6
River Yare	23-04	1
Rudyard Lake	20-14	1
Smiths Lake	27-12	5
South Drove	20-12	1
Southerton Lagoon	22-00	1
Suffork Water Park	21-06	1
Sywell Reservoir	20-01	1
St. Johns	21-00	1
Staffordshire Reservoir	32-02	11
Stanford Reservoir	20-10	1
Staunton Harold Reservoir	25-04	3
Stoneacres	23-04	2
Sussex Lake	41-04	1
Swangey Pit	33-14	1
Tong Mere	30-09	8
Wintons Heron Lake	32-04	2
Wintons Kingfisher Lake	20-04	1
Yorkshire Lake	24-04	2

No of Venues 56 **TOTAL 165**